THE ART OF
JOHN BOLTON

Short Bio

John Bolton spends his days locked inside his eerie prop-and-dead-bug filled studio in North London, England. After receiving his diploma in illustration and design he contributed to all kinds of famous (and infamous) British magazines and was subsequently commissioned to produce covers and artwork for book publishers. He began working in comics in 1980. An award-winning artist who has worked on graphic novels and prestige format books with Clive Barker, Chris Claremont, Christopher Fowler, Neil Gaiman, Sam Raimi, Anne Rice and others, he has handled assignments for every major publisher in the comics field.

John's ethereal vampire-women and magical creatures have made his work much sought after by collectors. His interest in the stylish and bizarre elements of the horror/fantasy genres is evident throughout his work. His cover artwork features some of the most recognizable and distinctive designs in comic-book history.

Introduction by Neil Gaiman

DRAWN IN DARKNESS

Late in the afternoon, John Mirabilis Bolton picks up his red leather gas mask and walks down the path from his Crouch End house to the concrete bomb shelter that serves him as a studio.

The gas mask, which has been blessed by the Pope, the Dalai Lama and the Supreme Sanguifex of the Clinical Brethren, is, Bolton claims, "essential to the process". If he is not wearing it he cannot paint.

When asked whether it cuts down on his field of vision Bolton smiles, shyly. "Only in reality" he explains. "I may lose vision, but I can see so much more with it on. It's shamanic, I suppose."

Bolton must be alone while he paints.

He starts each working day, he states, with no ideas whatsoever. "The subjects of the paintings need to come to me", he says hesitantly. "You see, I have no imagination."

He is being precise here. The subjects of his paintings seek him out. They know where to find him. Bolton sits in his studio grinding paints, preparing his blank canvasses, all alone; when night falls he takes a taper and lights a few of the huge dark candles, melted now, if imagination amends them, into the shapes of fantastic beasts: turtles and stonefish, dragons and demon-heads, and he waits to see who, or what, he will be painting that night.

"The candles are my only superstition", says Bolton who was made a Freeman and Servitor of Crouch End in the 1996 Honours List; if you encounter John Bolton within the bounds of Crouch End, you must remove your hat and may not, by tradition, speak to him unless he speaks to you first. With the honour comes the right to cull the wild ermine, the small stoat-like beasts that plagued Crouch End long ago, when it was still a tiny village to the northwest of London, but have not been seen in the borough in living memory; even so, Bolton wears a traditional silver ermine knife at his belt. "When they return", he says, with a grin, "I'll be ready for them."

The subjects of his paintings come to him, mostly at night. They slip through the shadows and walk down the gravestone steps to his studio, moonlight making their skin glow with a pale luminosity, candle-light glinting in their eyes and on the sharpness of their teeth.

Is he scared of them? The artist shakes his head. "They come to me", he explains. "The process – the making real – is as important to them as it is to me. They need me. Why would they hurt me?" But has he never been scared? He looks down. "You cannot let them see that you are afraid. Who would they find to paint them if I was gone? Anyway", he adds, patting the silver ermine-skinner on his belt, "I have a knife." Does he talk to them while he paints them? He does not answer. Instead he begins to light candles.

How do they find out about him? Is there a grapevine among the naked and undead of London, a word passed along from pale vampire girl to restless satyr to faceless lamia? Bolton declines to speculate. "If they did not come to me, I would have nothing to paint", he says. "I am grateful, and leave it there."

What if he wished to paint something else? Fruit bowls or flowers? What then? He shivers, and shakes his head, and says nothing.

A yellow newspaper clipping, cut from a May 1965 copy of the *News of the World* and taped to the lichen-stained wall of his studio, tells of Bolton's tutelage in painting at the hands of an ancient madman who claimed to have been Richard Dadd, the Victorian painter and parricide commonly believed to have died in 1886, seventy-five years, to the day, before Bolton was born. Bolton, however, refuses to discuss it. "It's water under the bridge", he says. "We must let the dead bury the dead. And I am grateful to all my teachers."

The sun is starting to set.

"You must leave now", says John Mirabilis Bolton, placing his red leather gas mask over his face, pulling the straps and buckles tight. "You would not want them to find you here." His voice is muffled behind the leather and the glass.

There are thirteen stone steps up from his studio to the mossy garden. In the trees at the bottom of the garden, something pale moves.

It is wisest not to look too closely.

Neil Gaiman, September 2, 1998

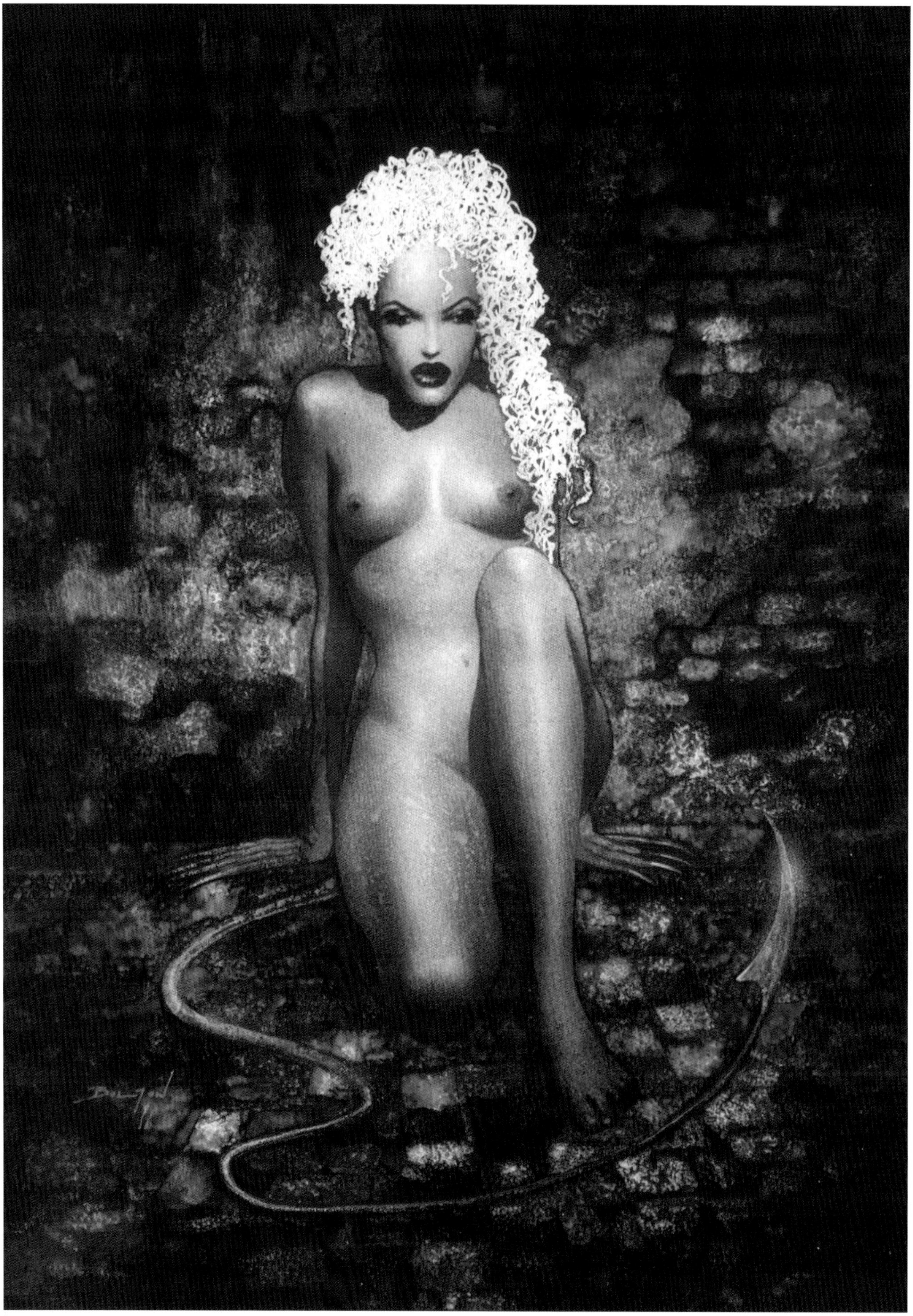

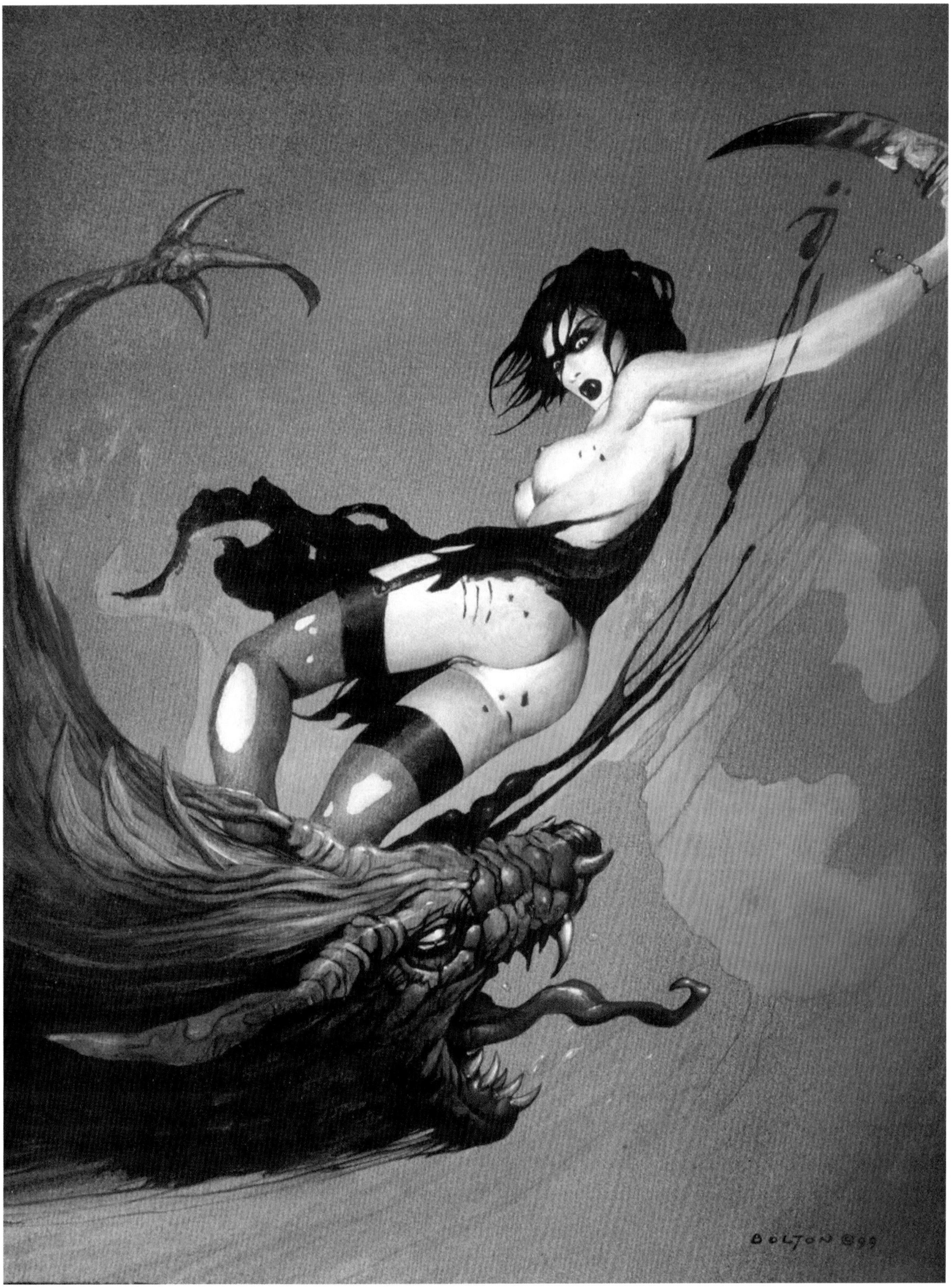
BOLTON ©99

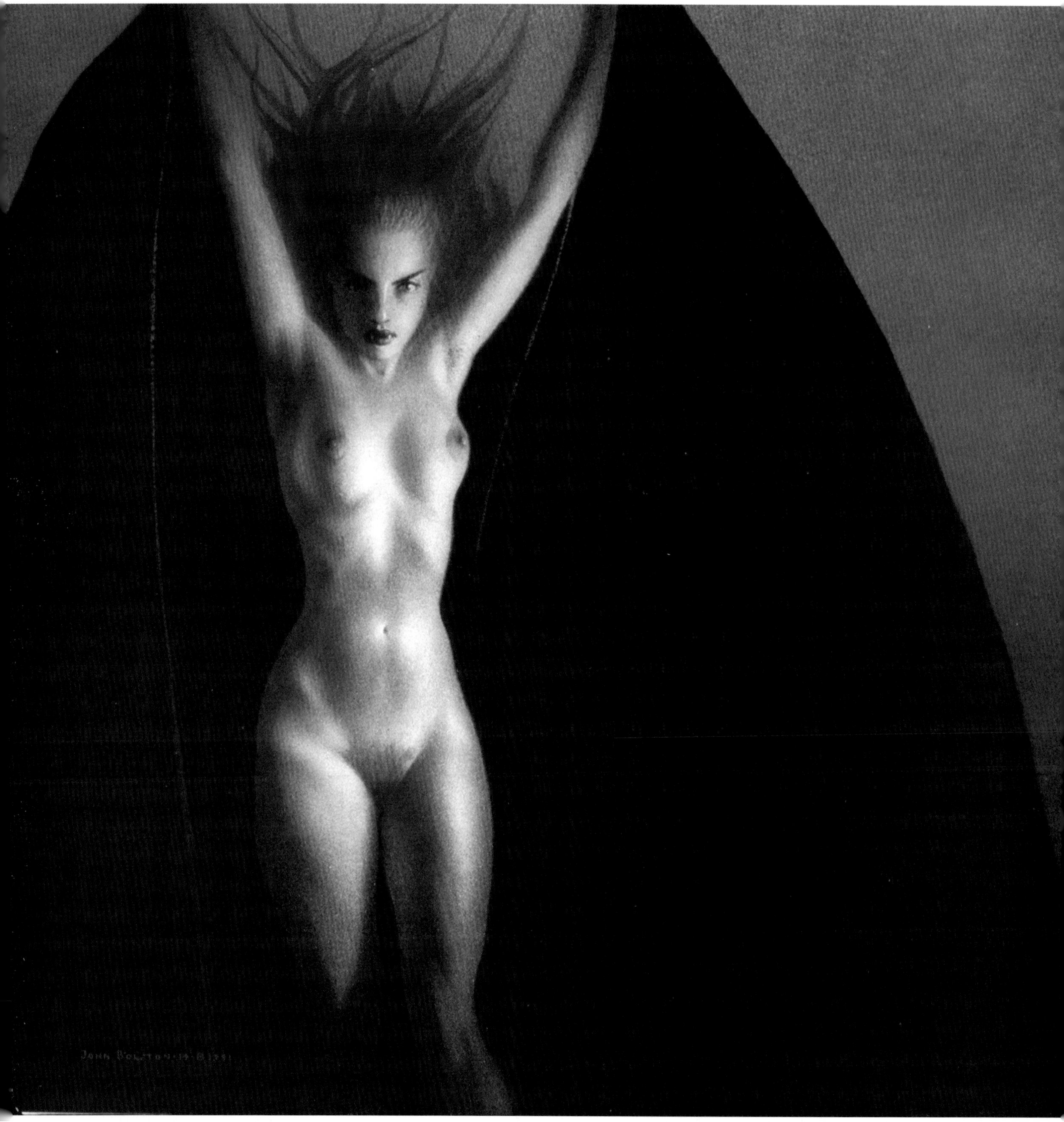

John Bolton

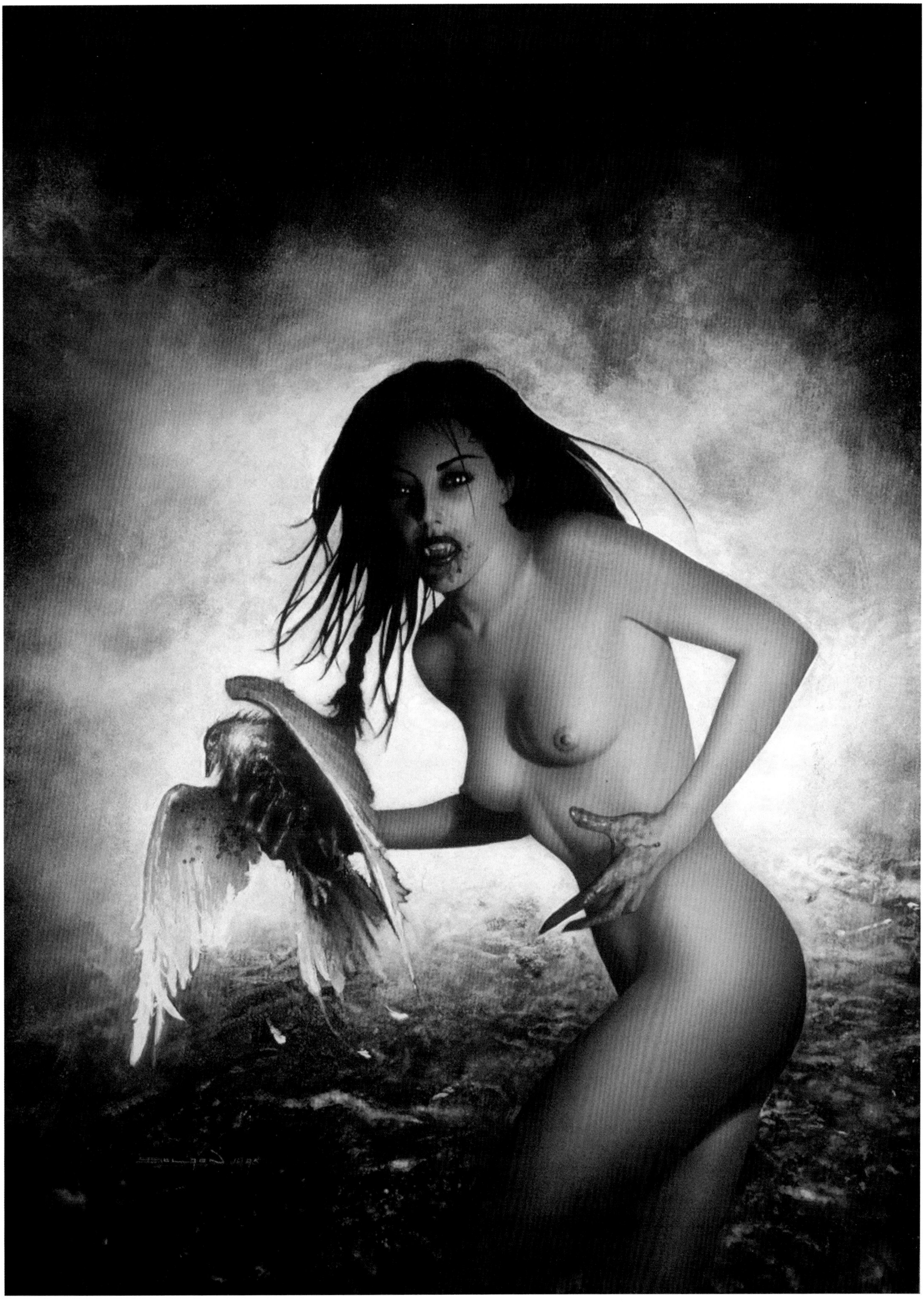

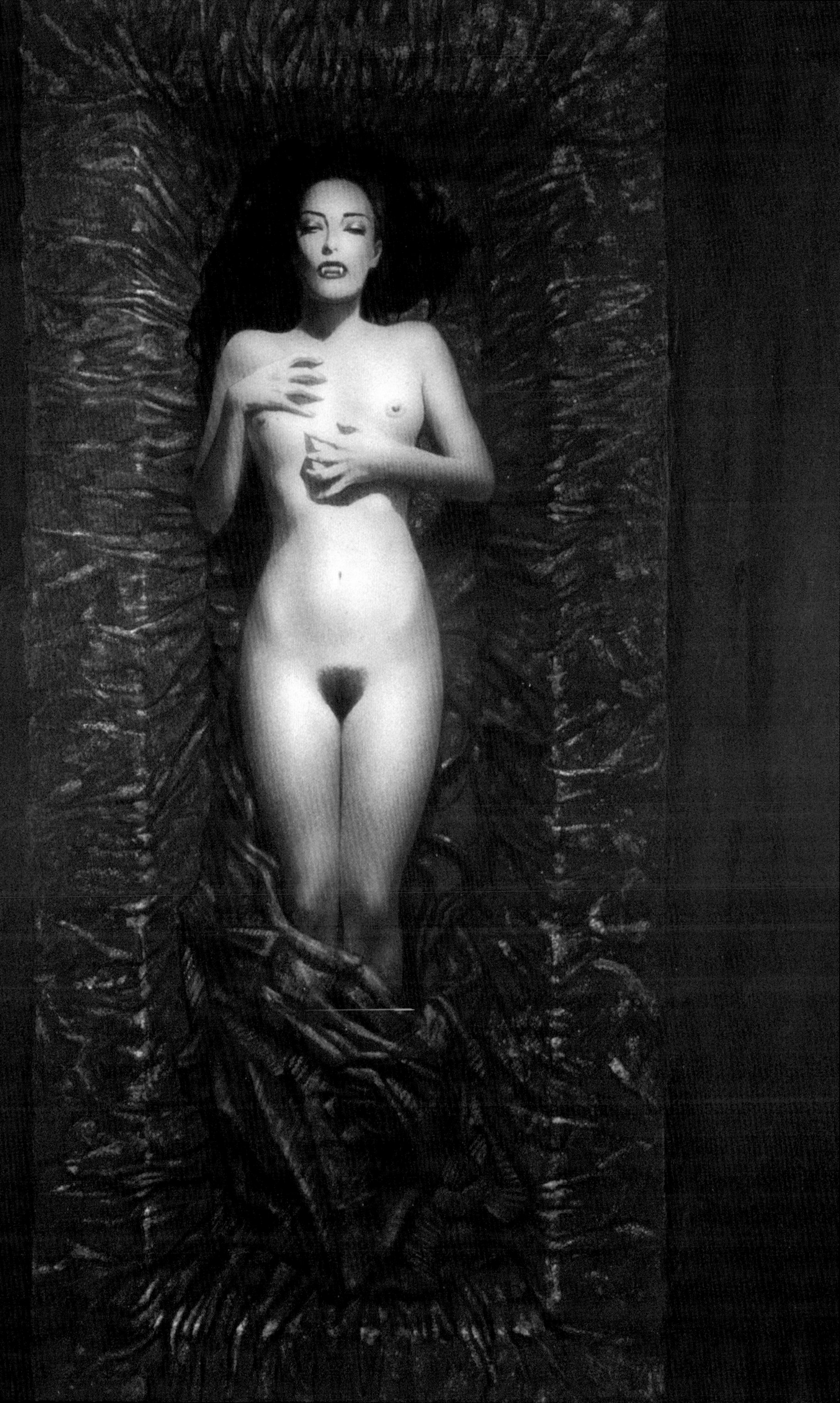

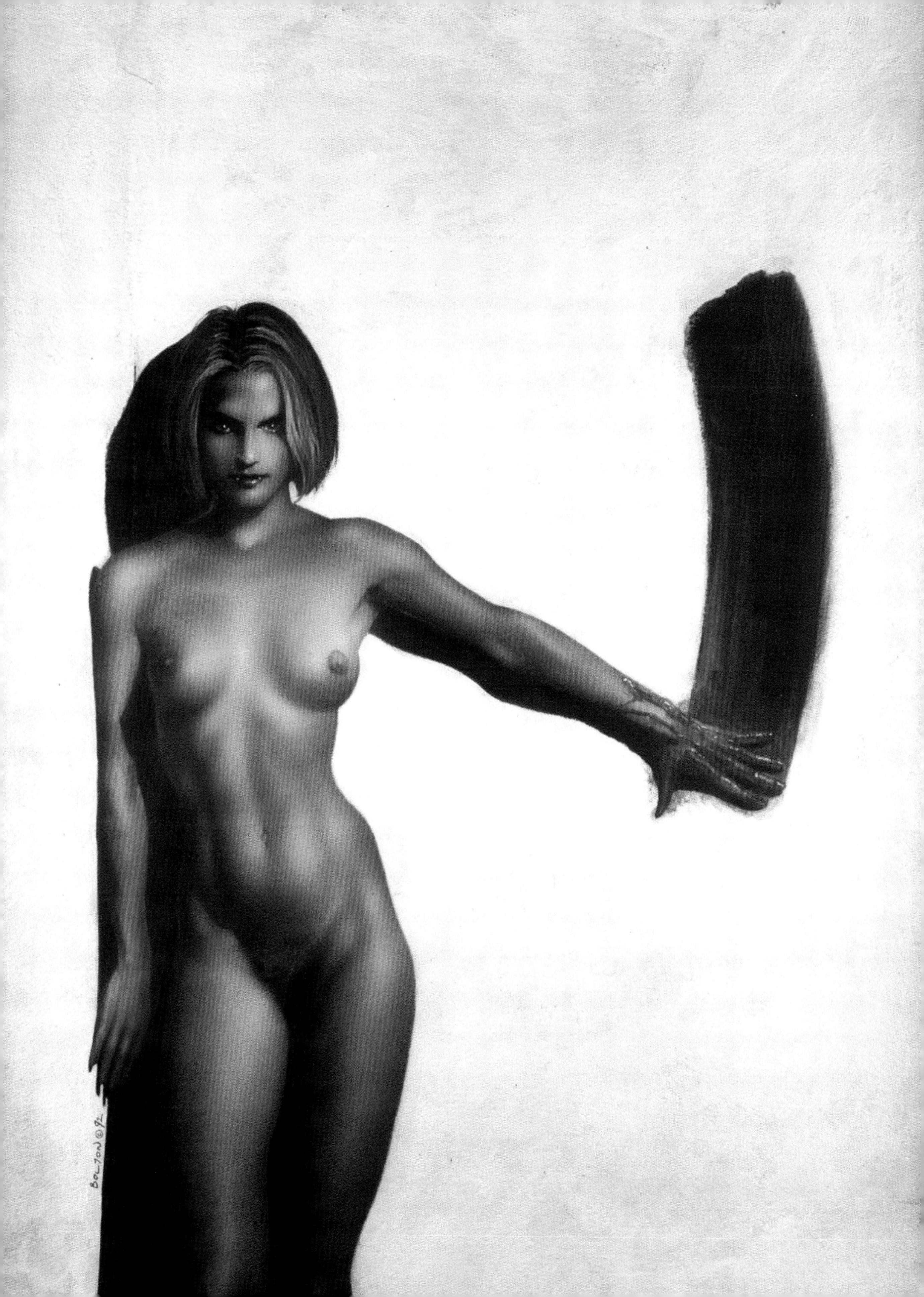
BOLTON ©92

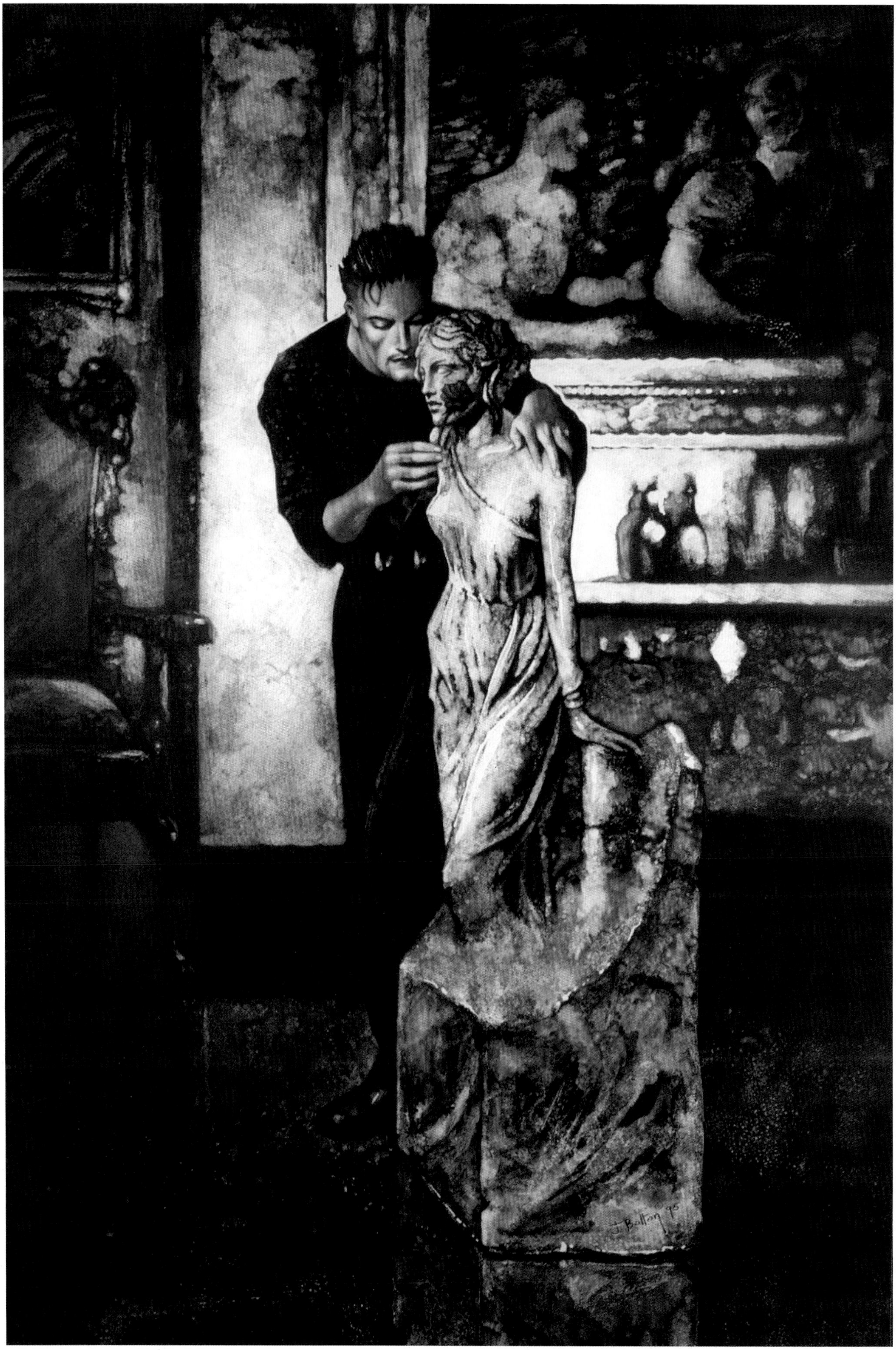

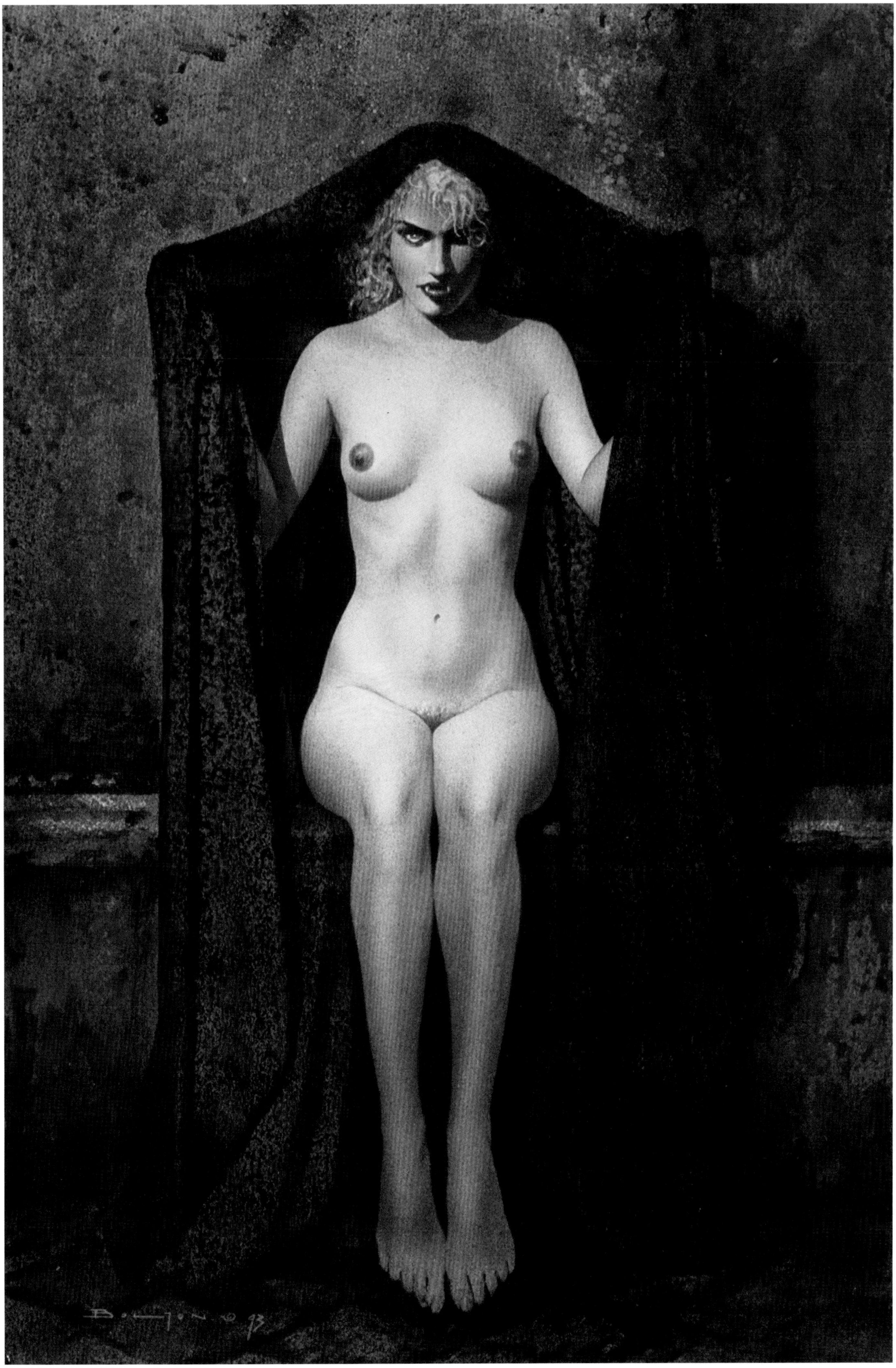

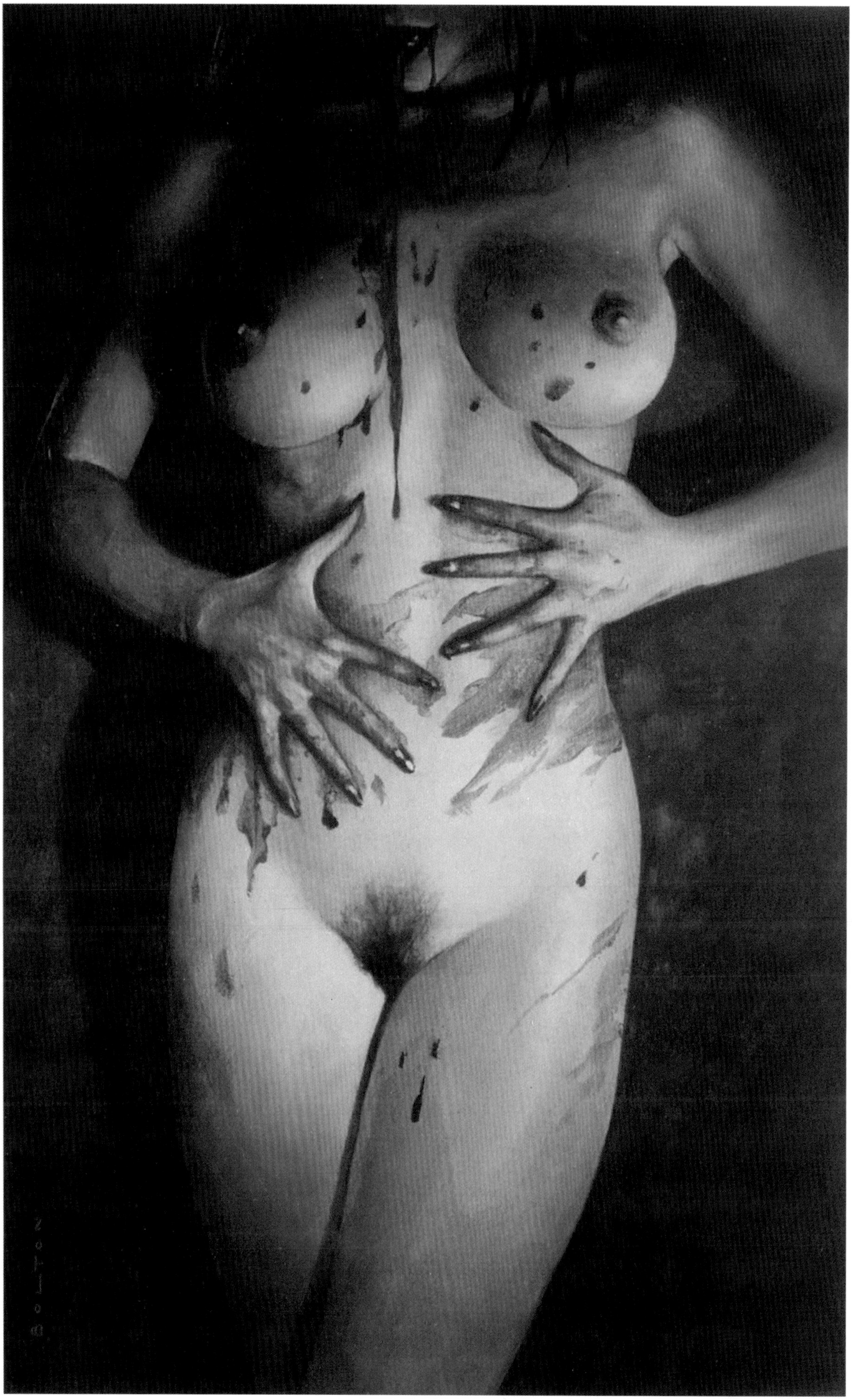
BOLTON

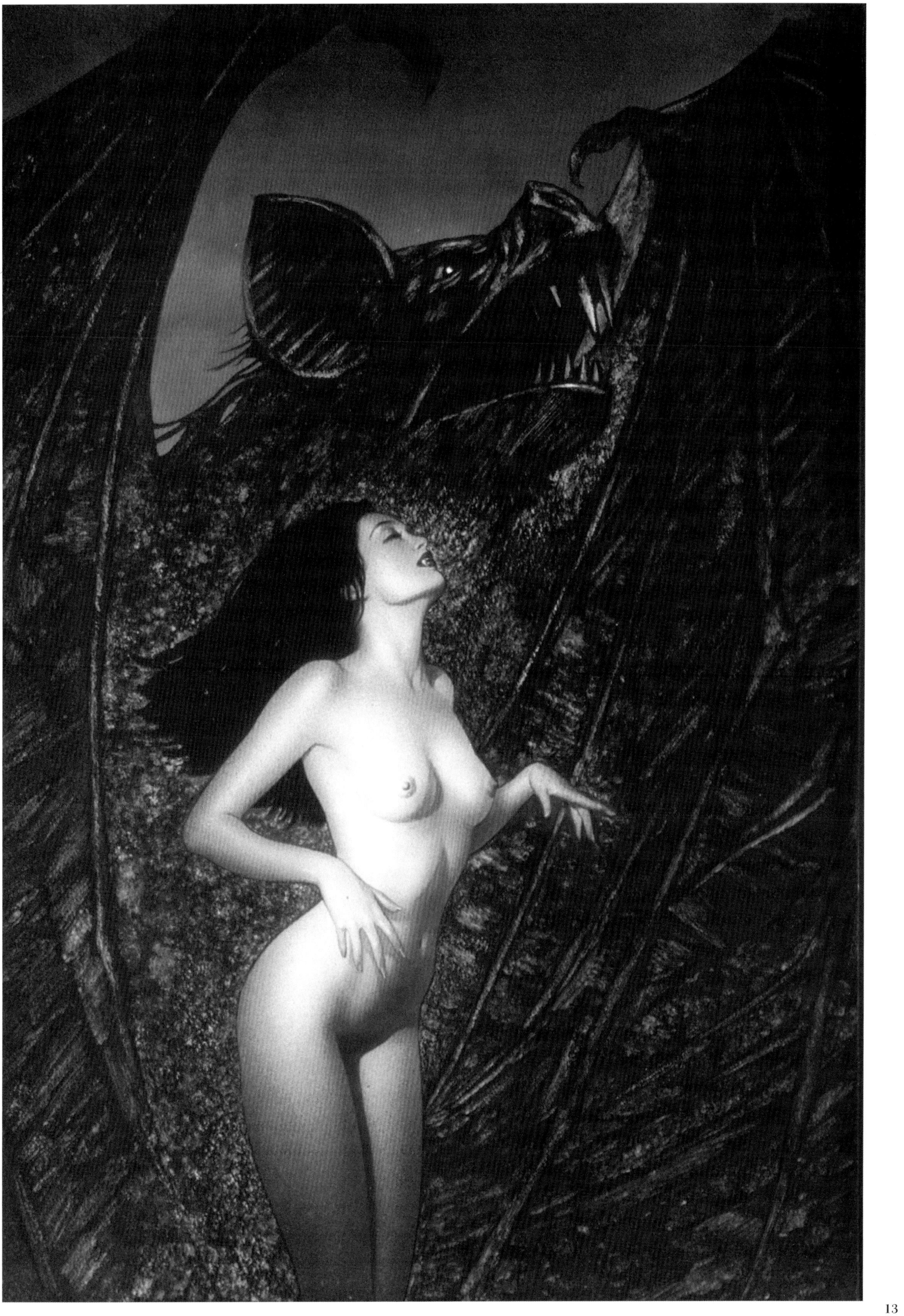

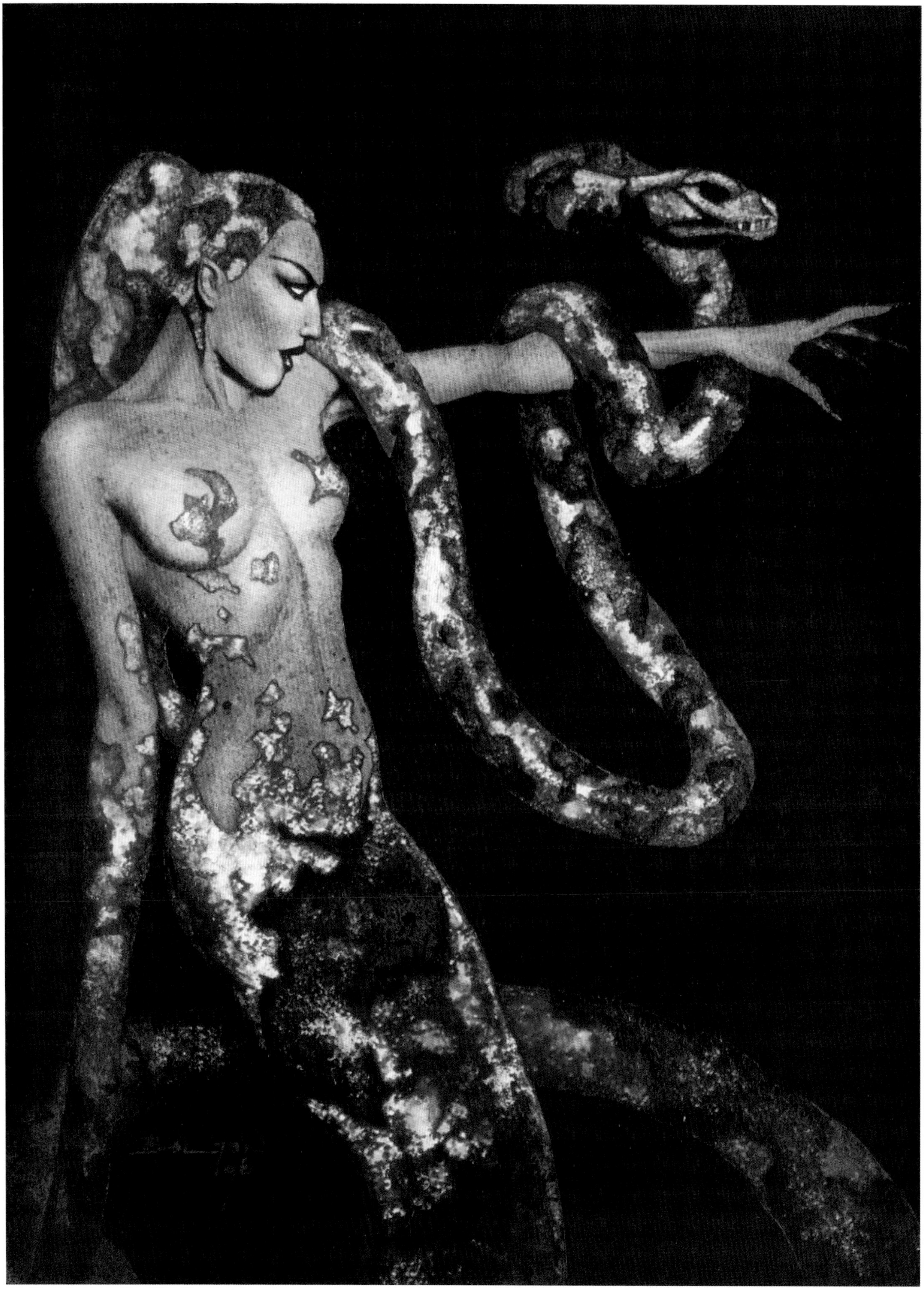

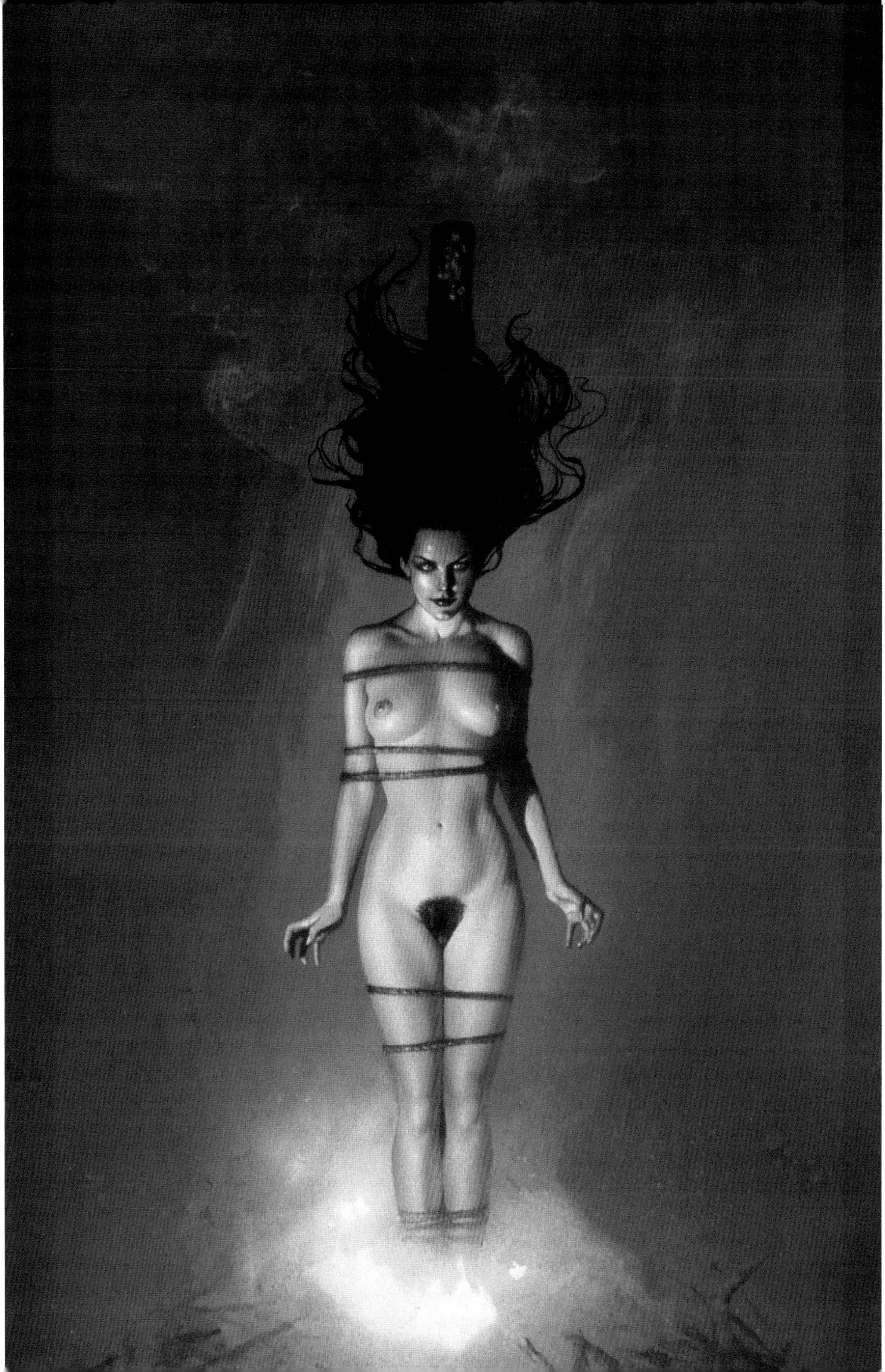

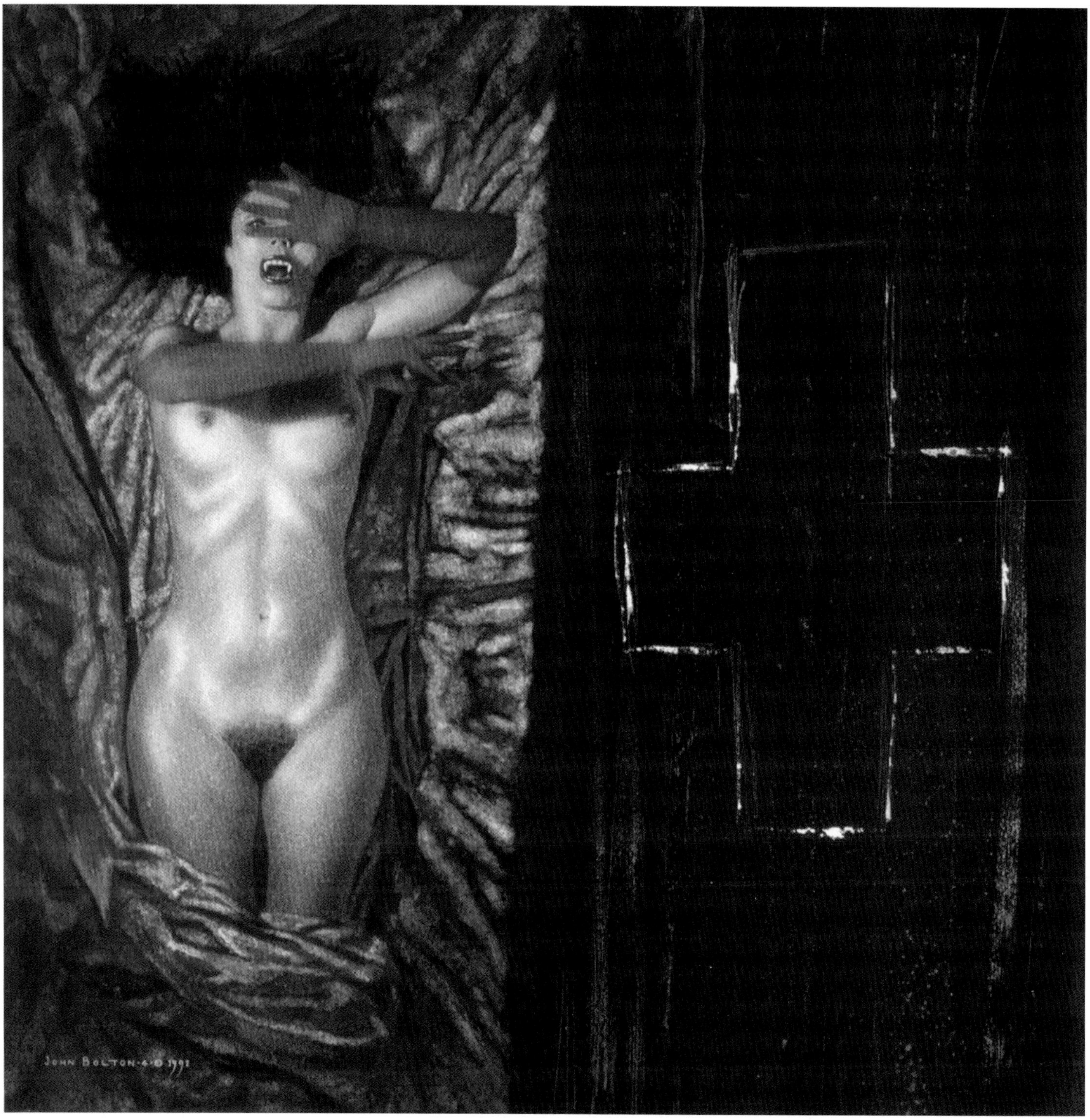
JOHN BOLTON

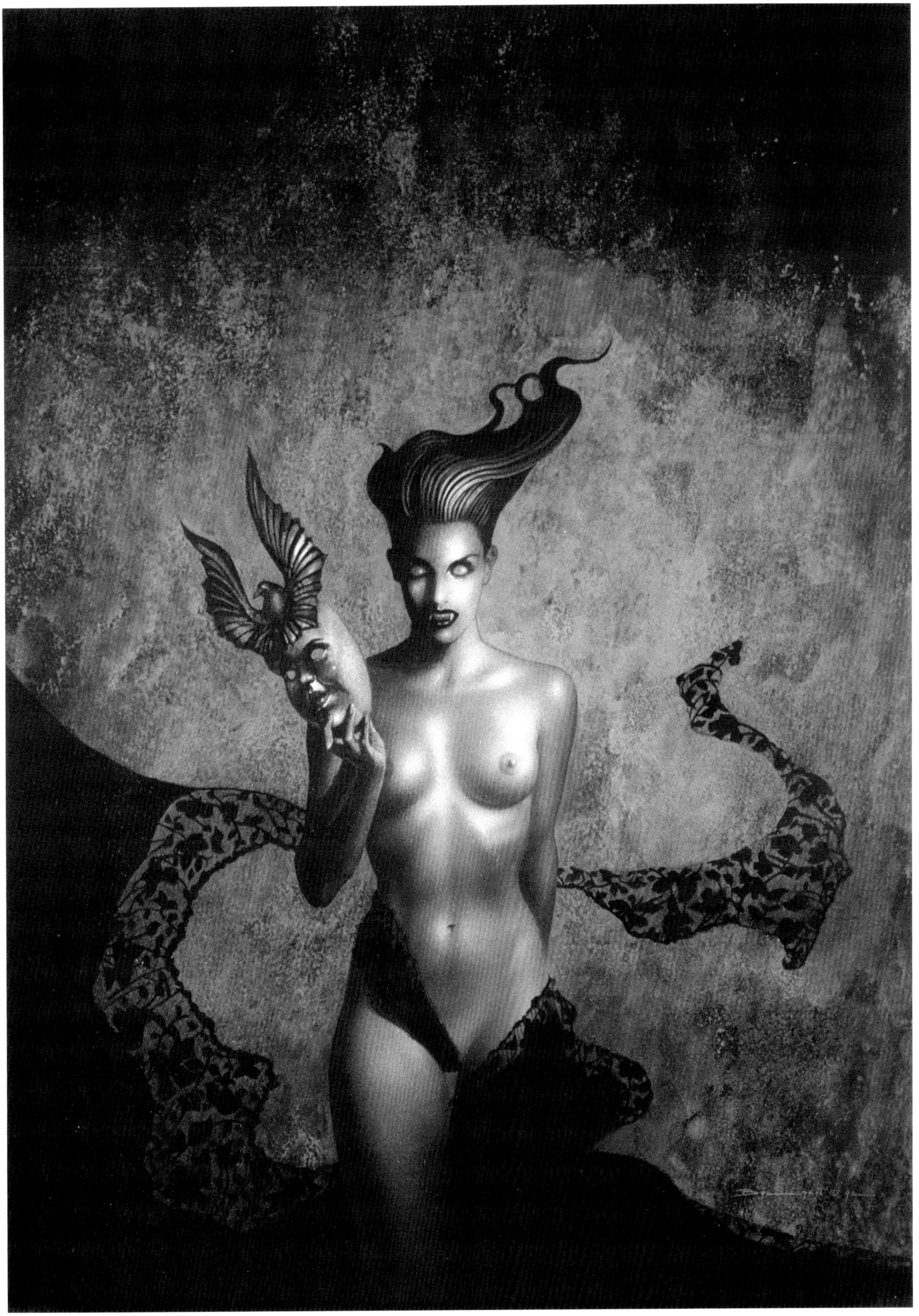

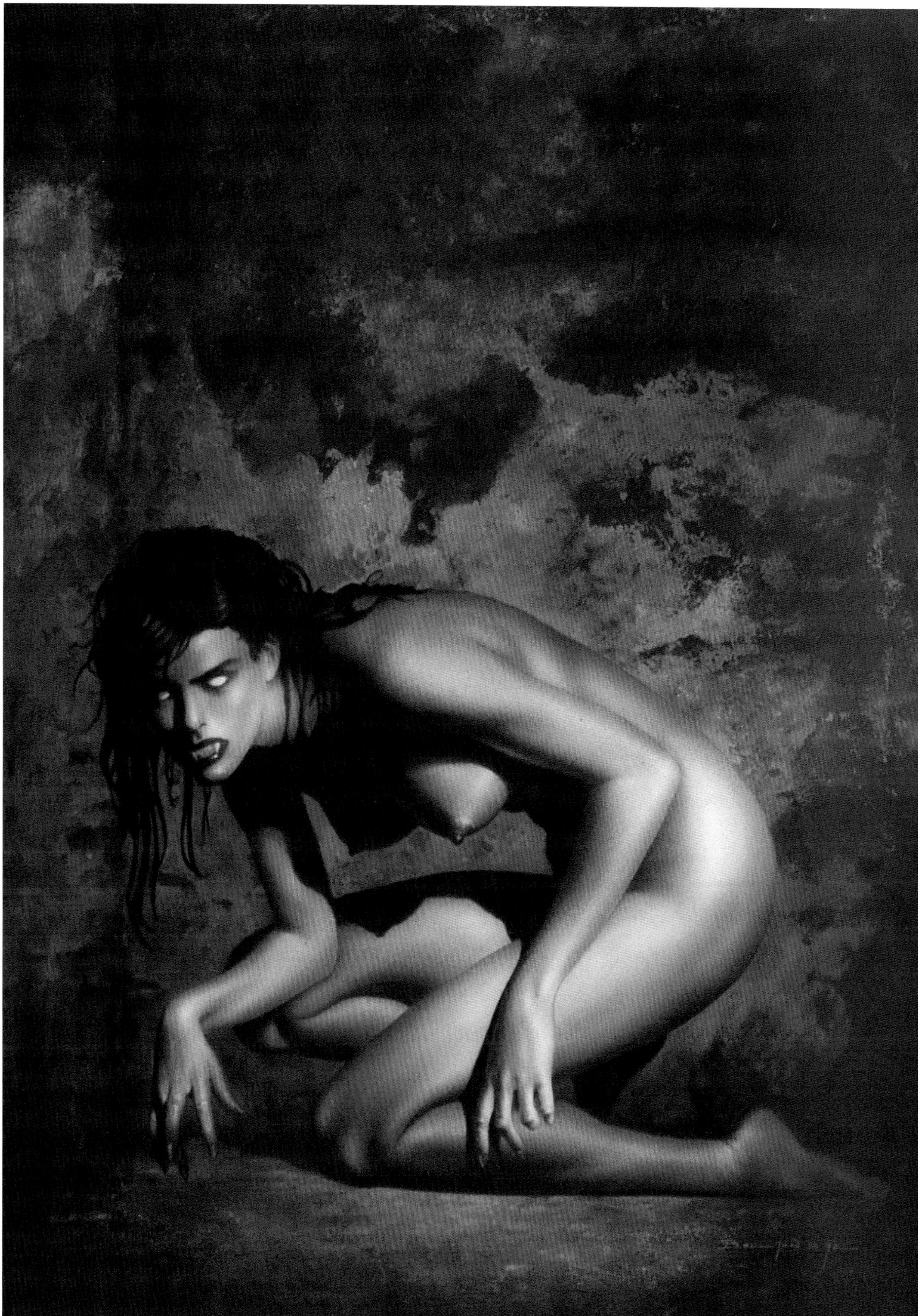

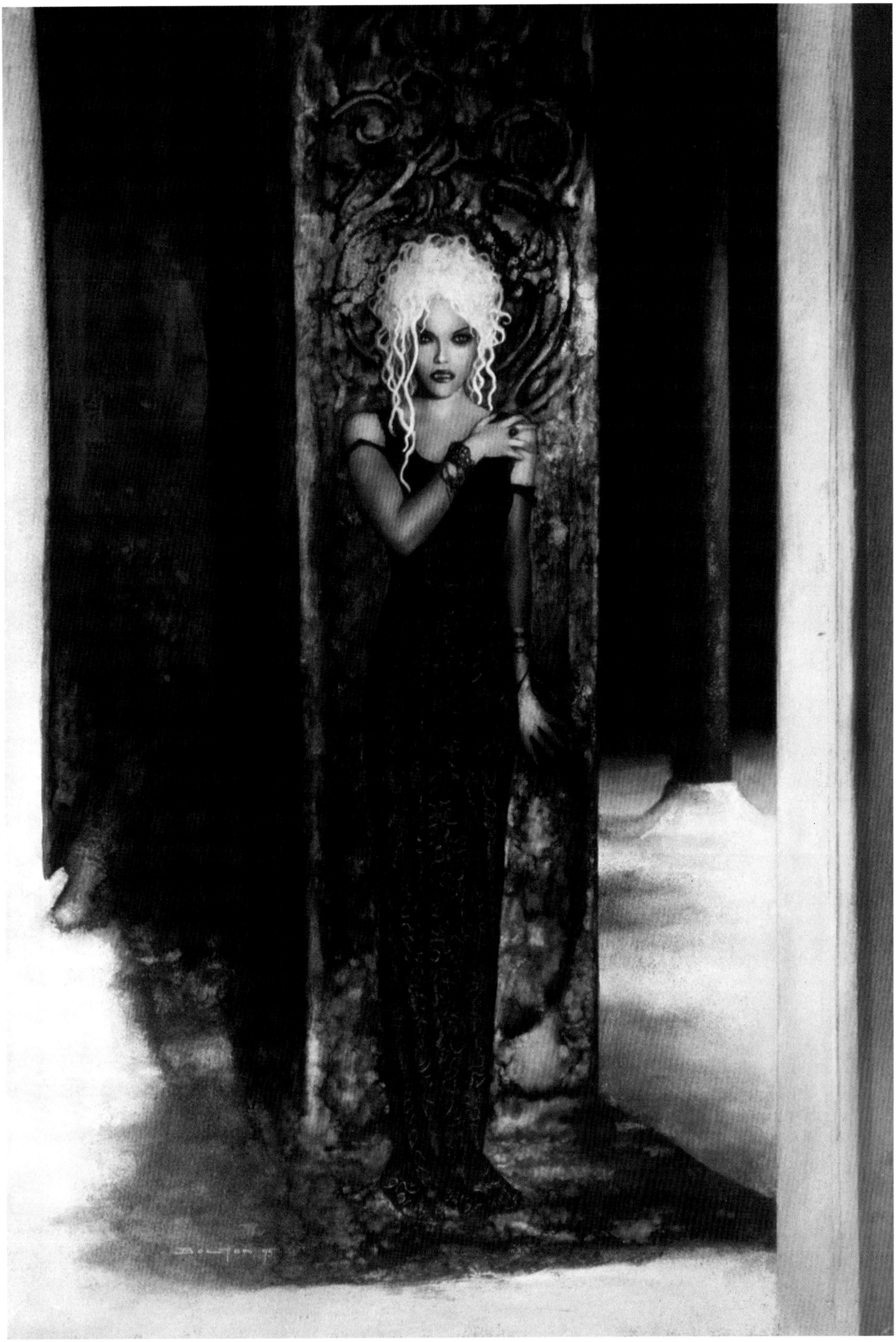

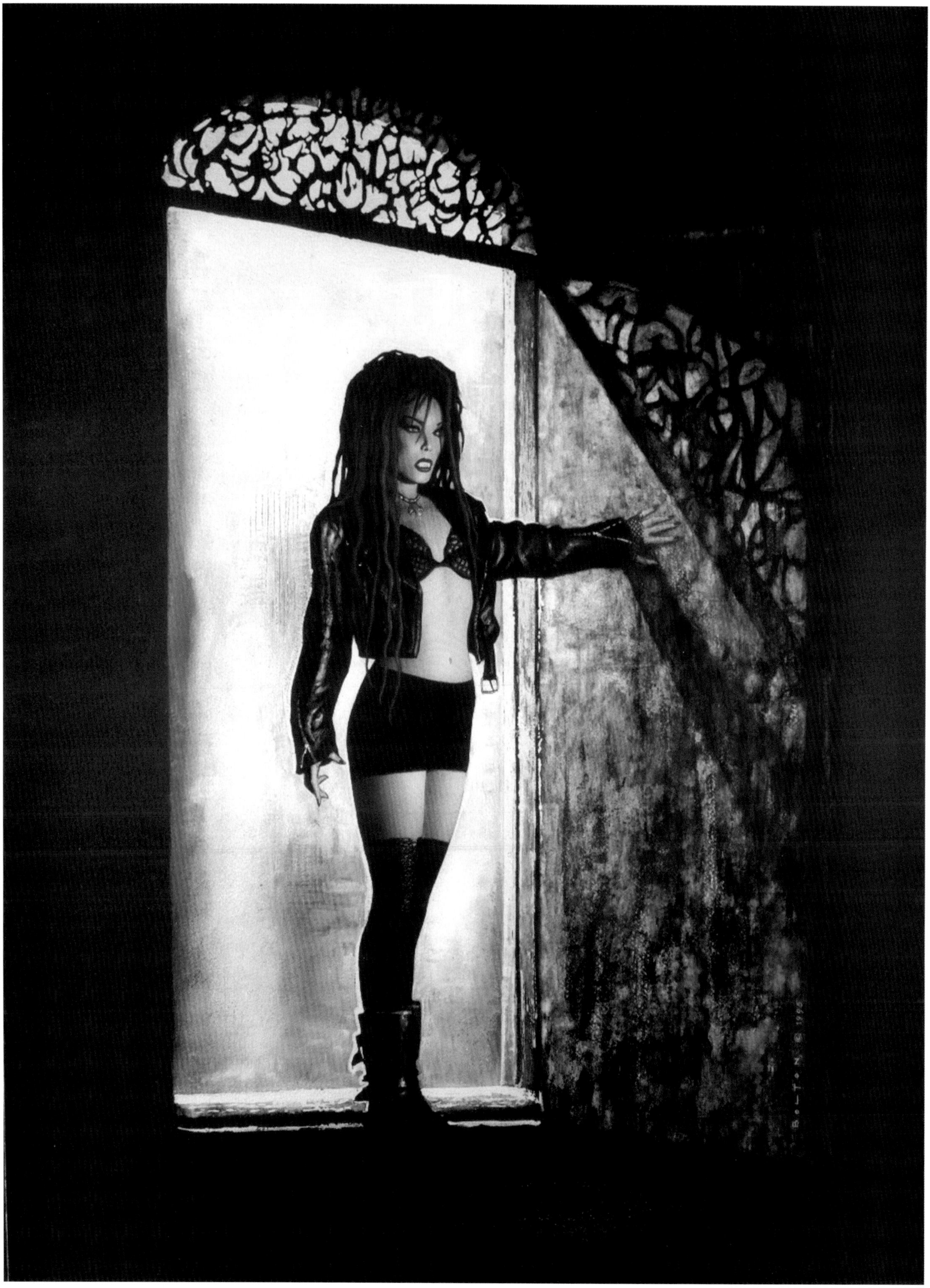

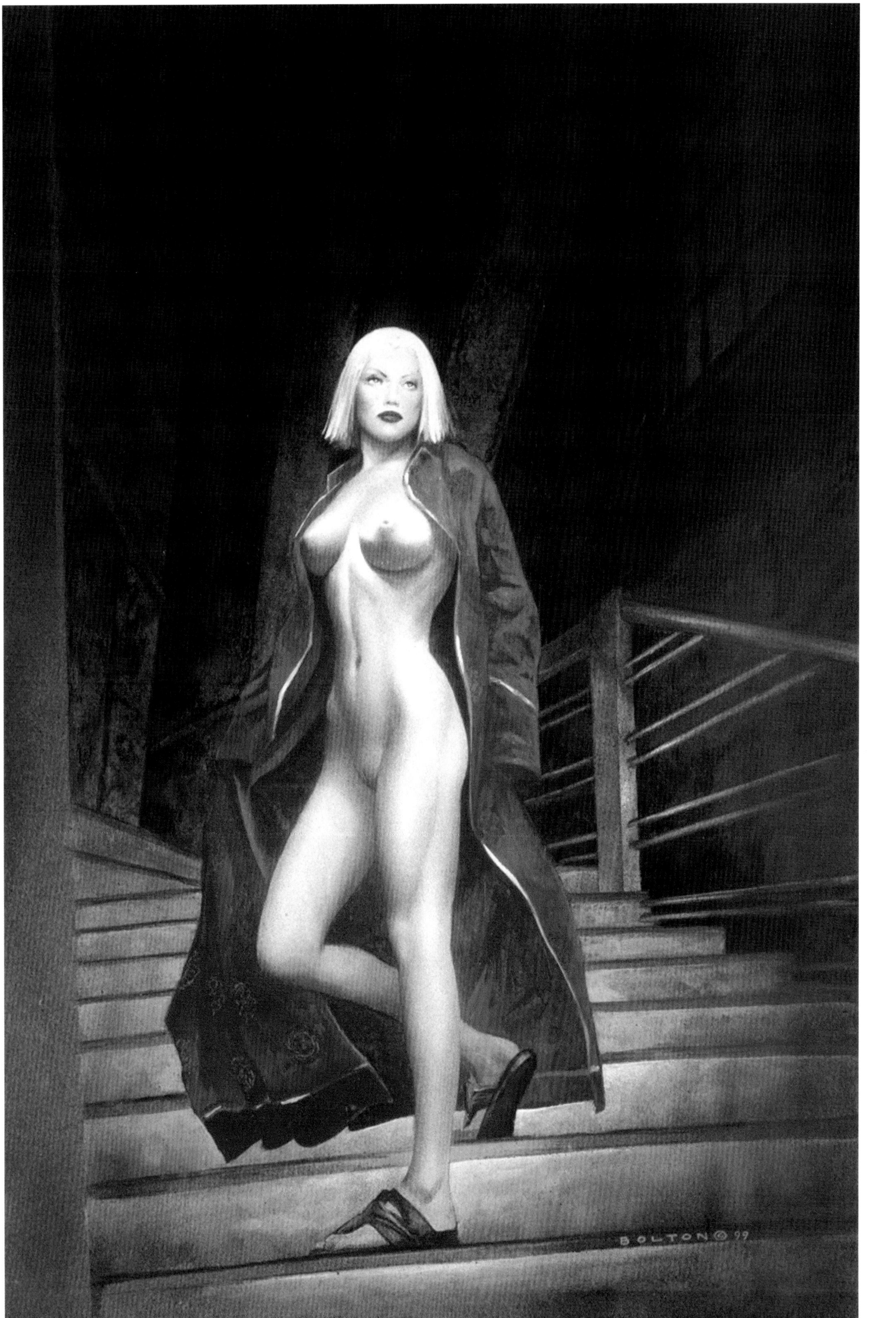
BOLTON © 99

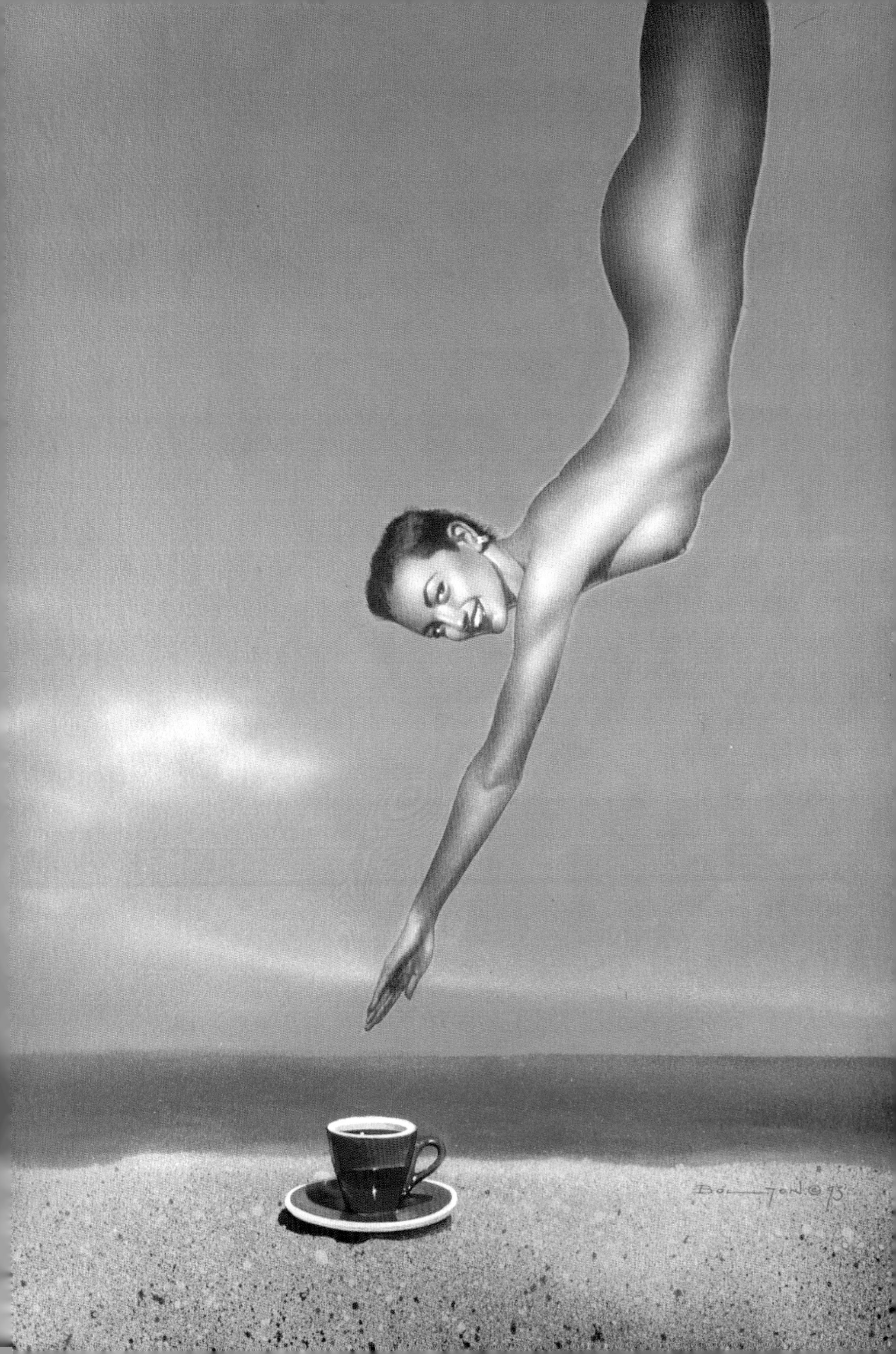

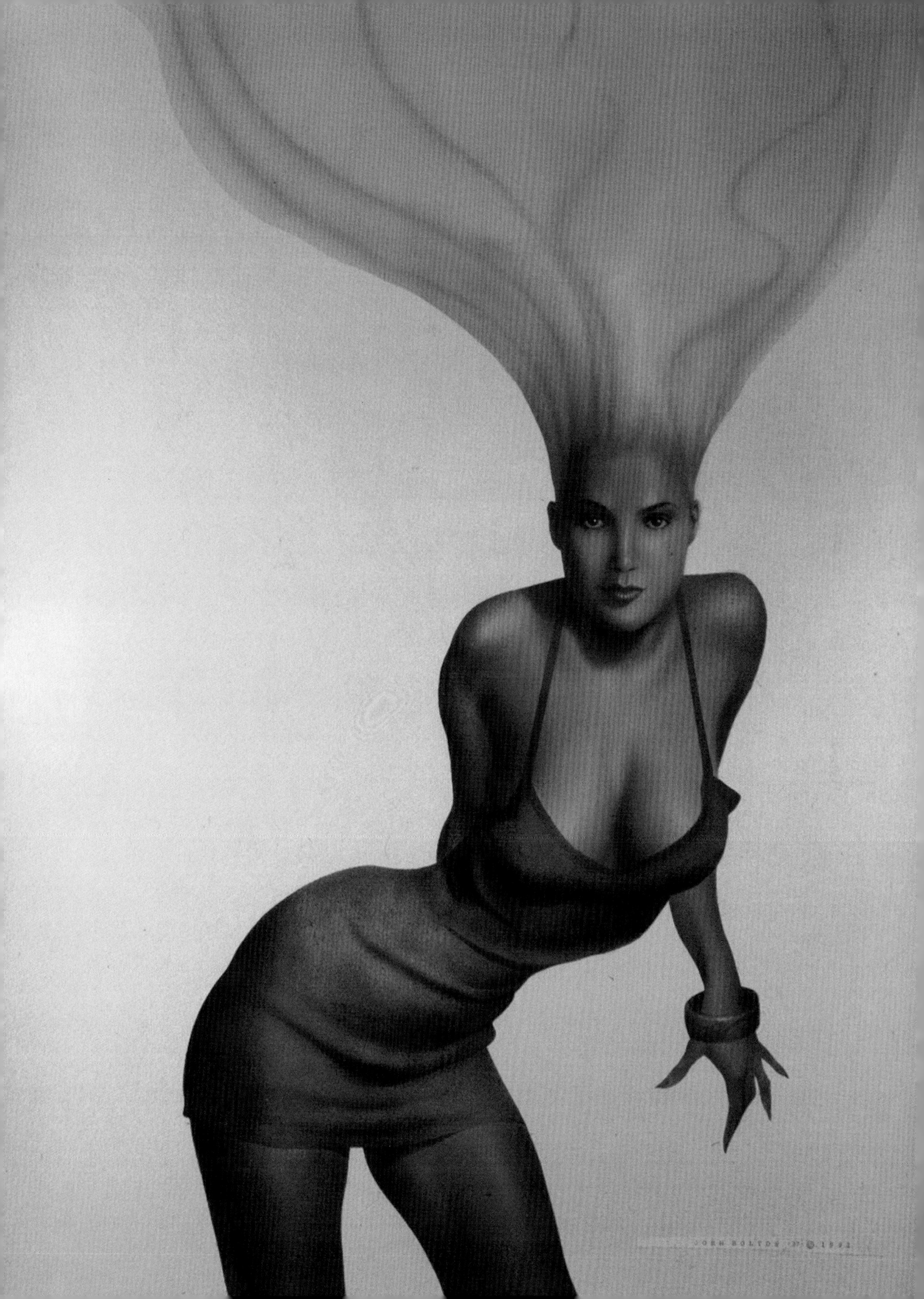

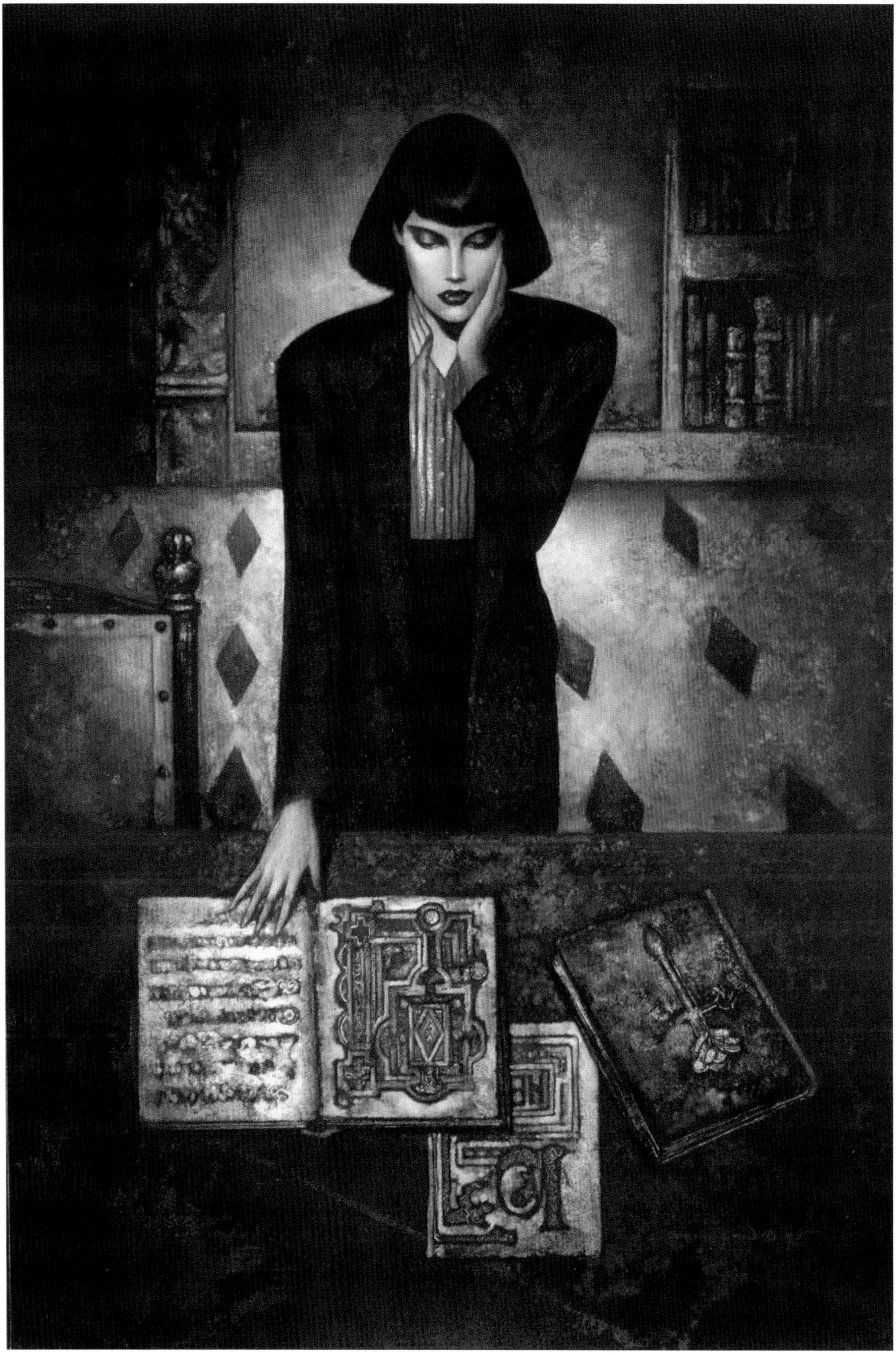

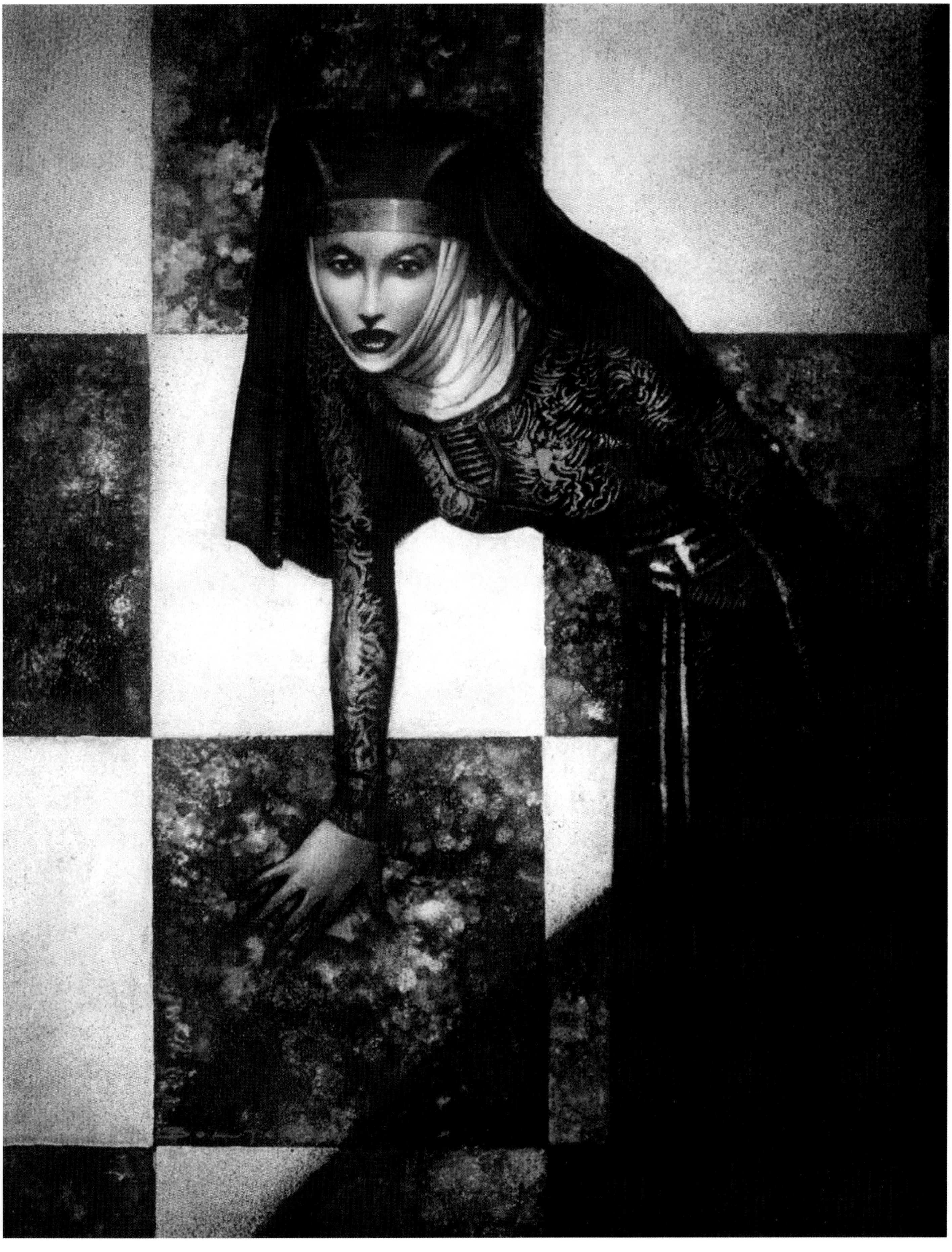

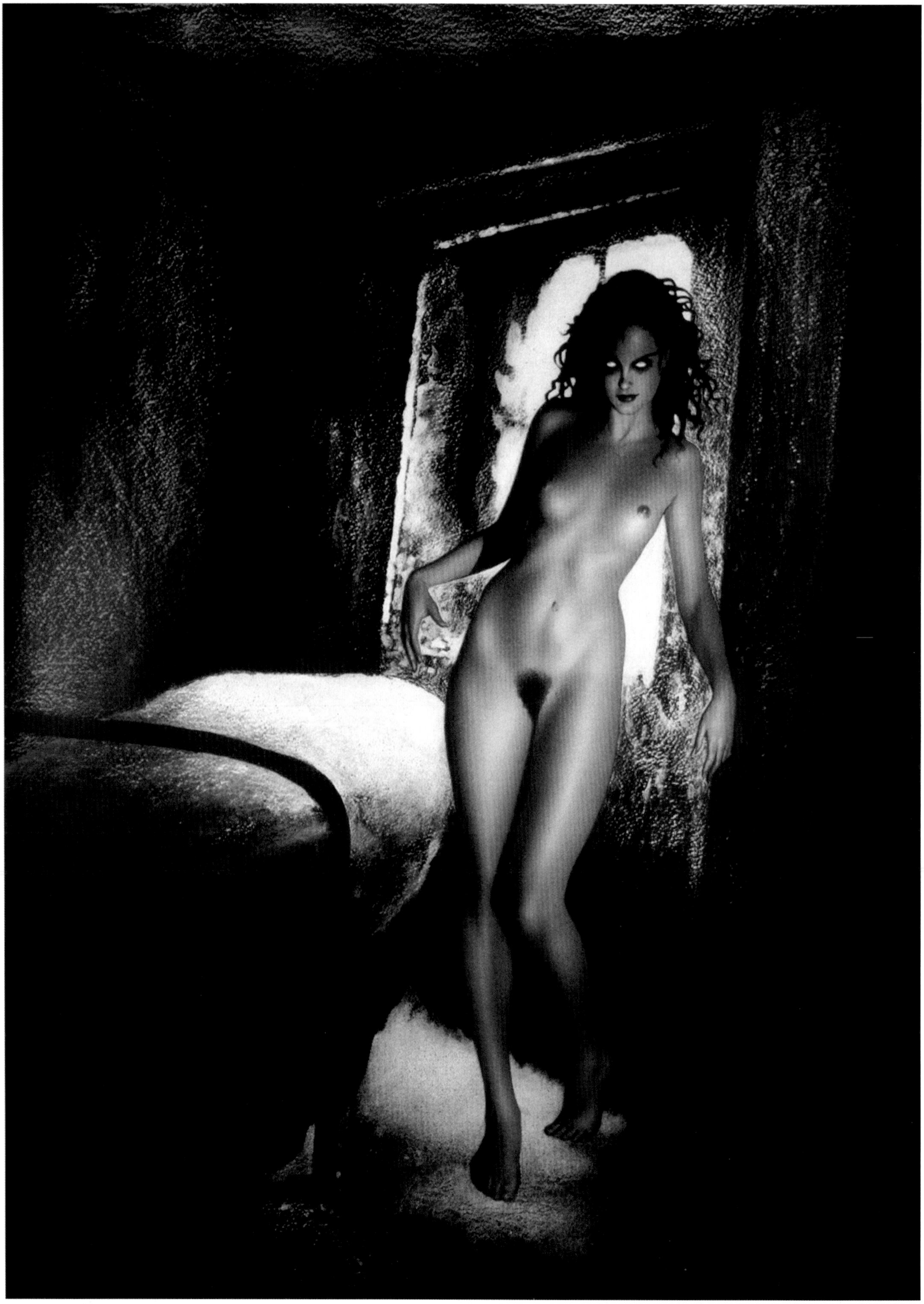

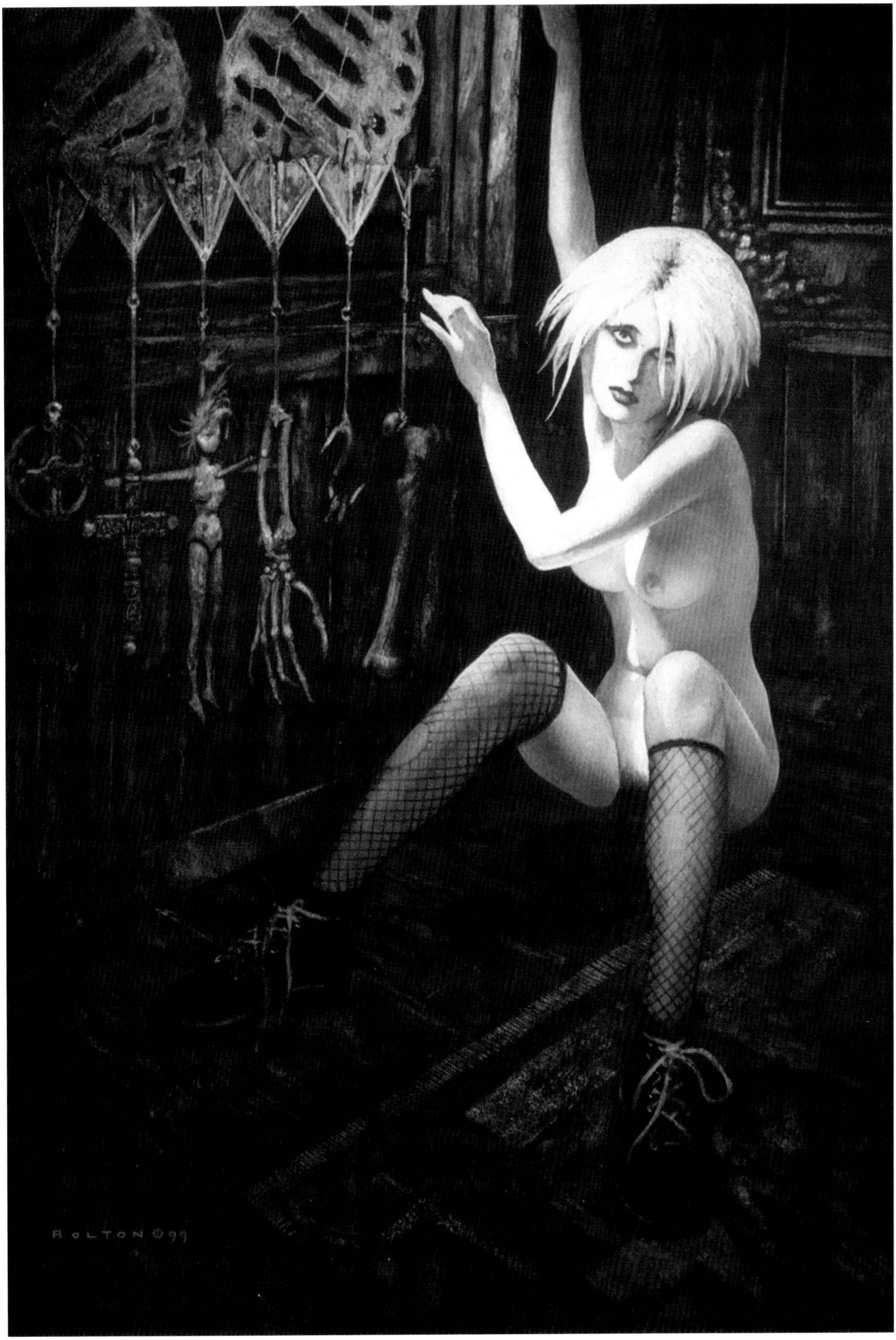
BOLTON ©99

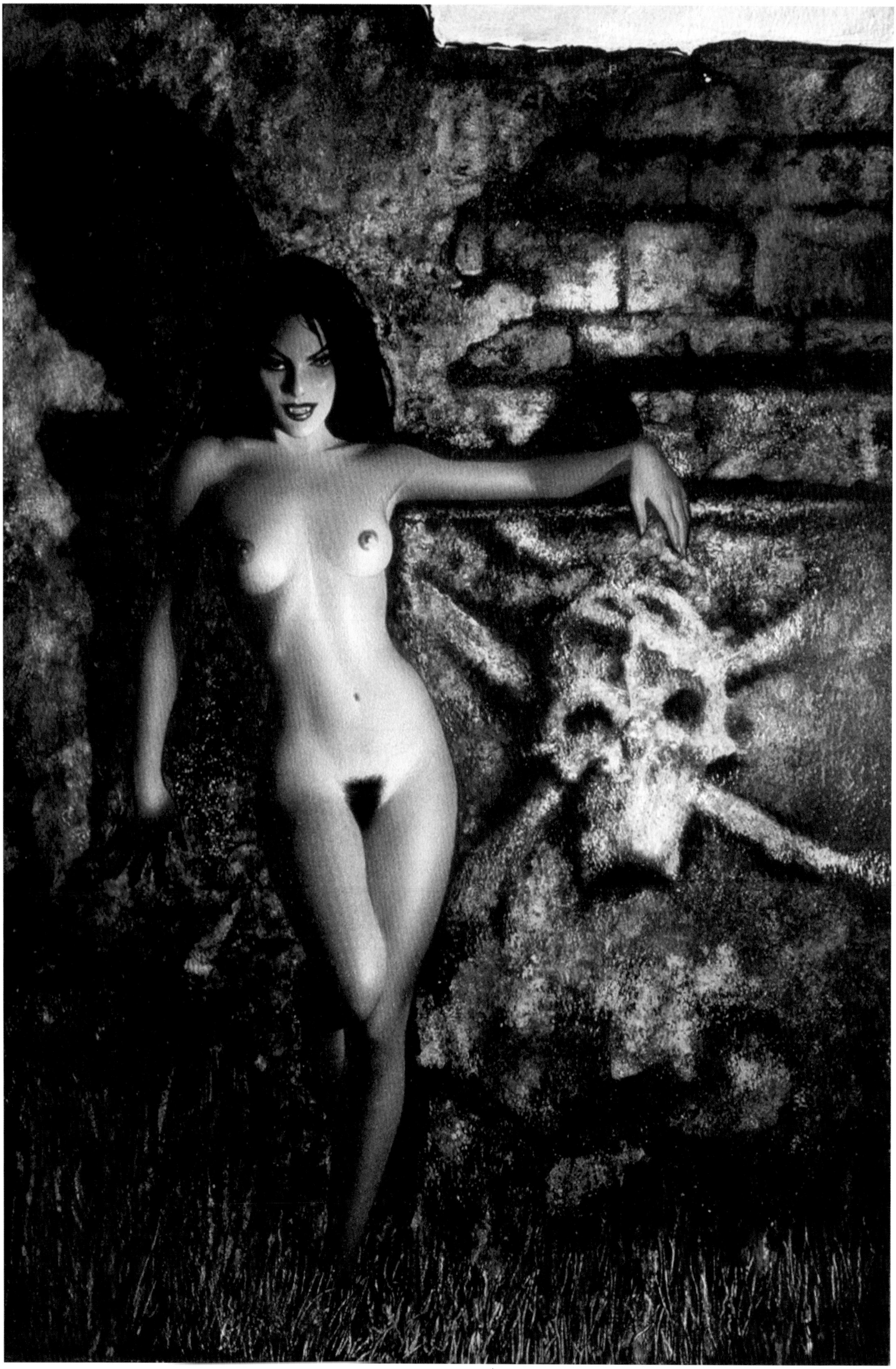

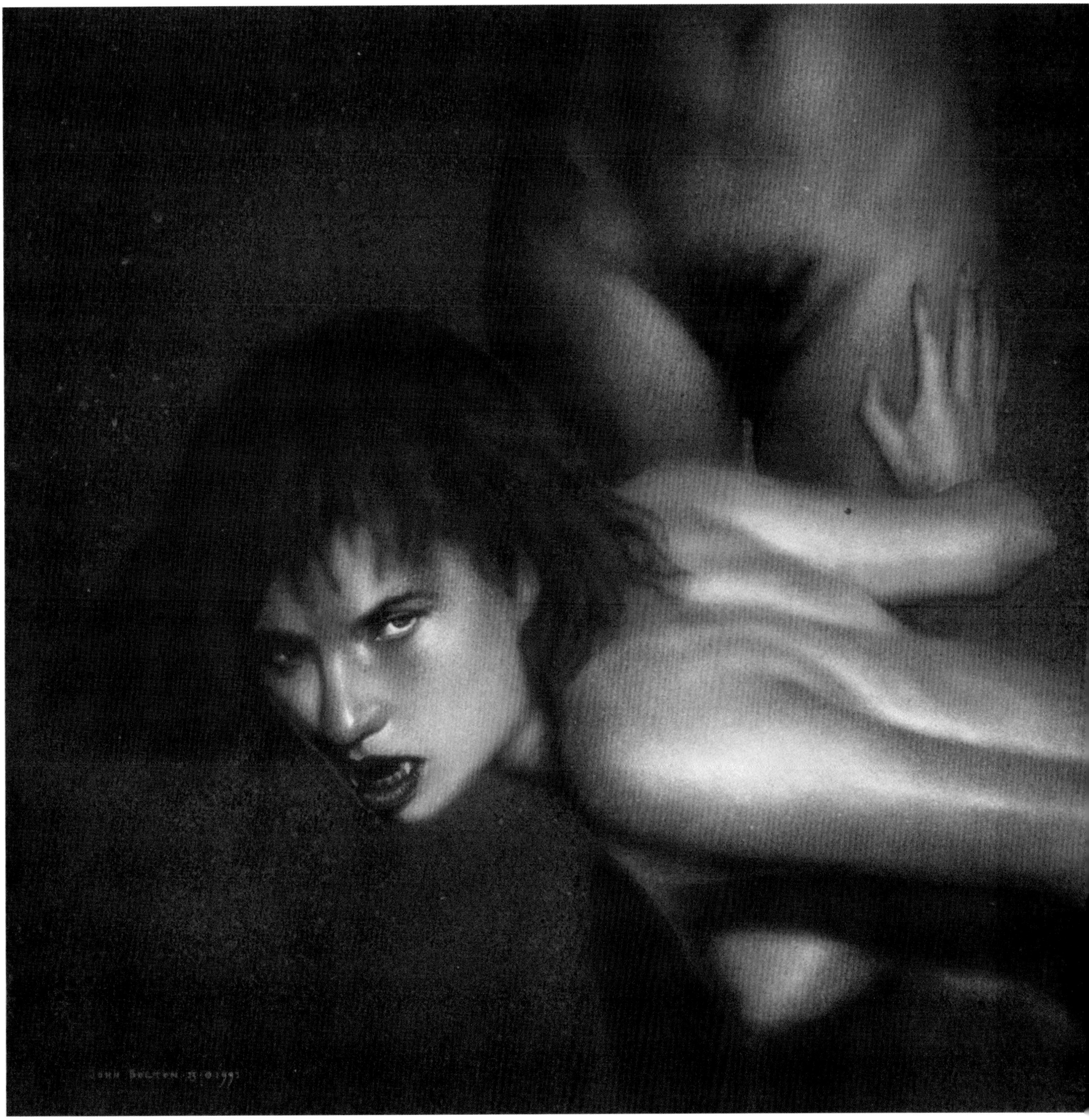

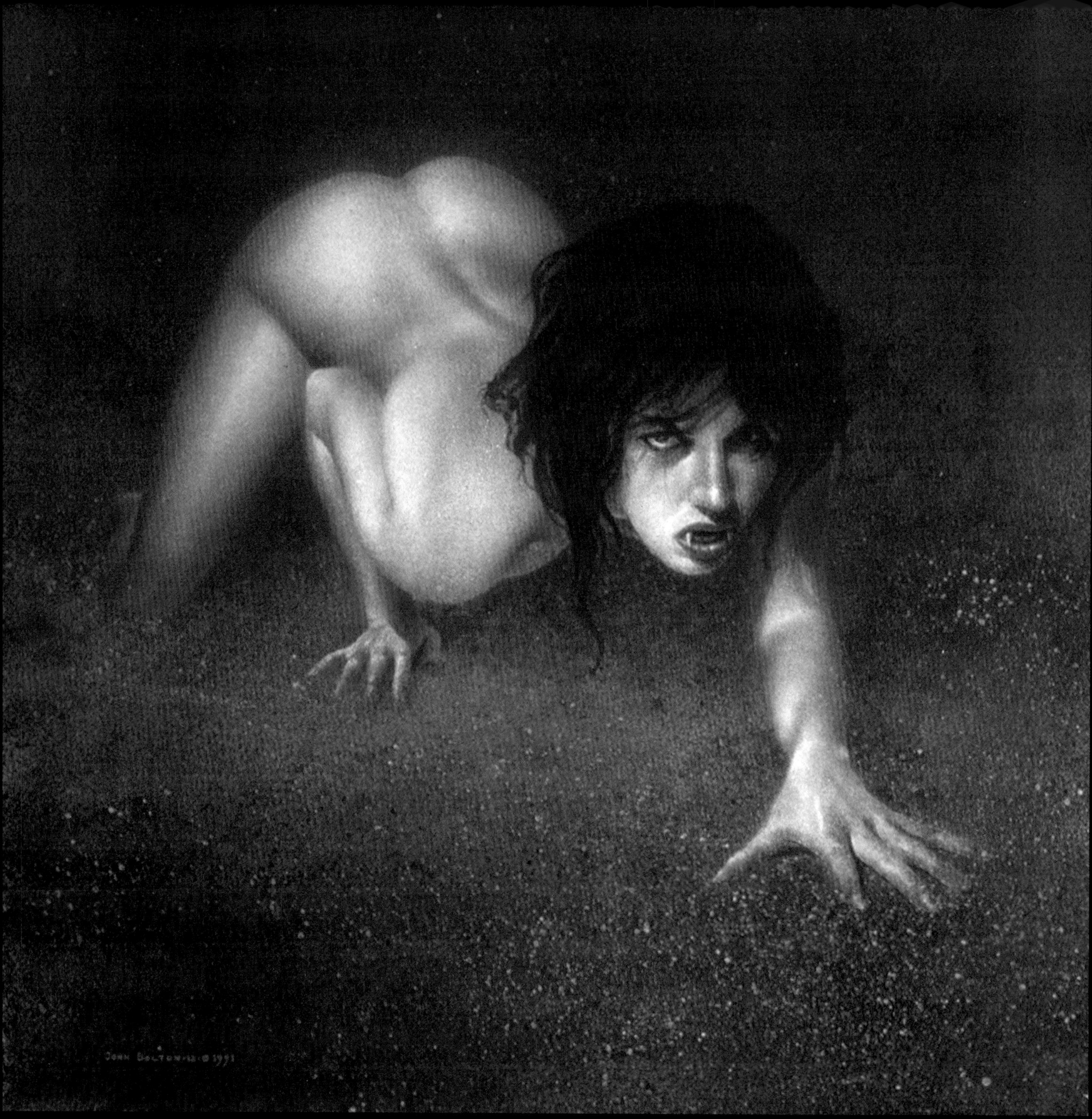

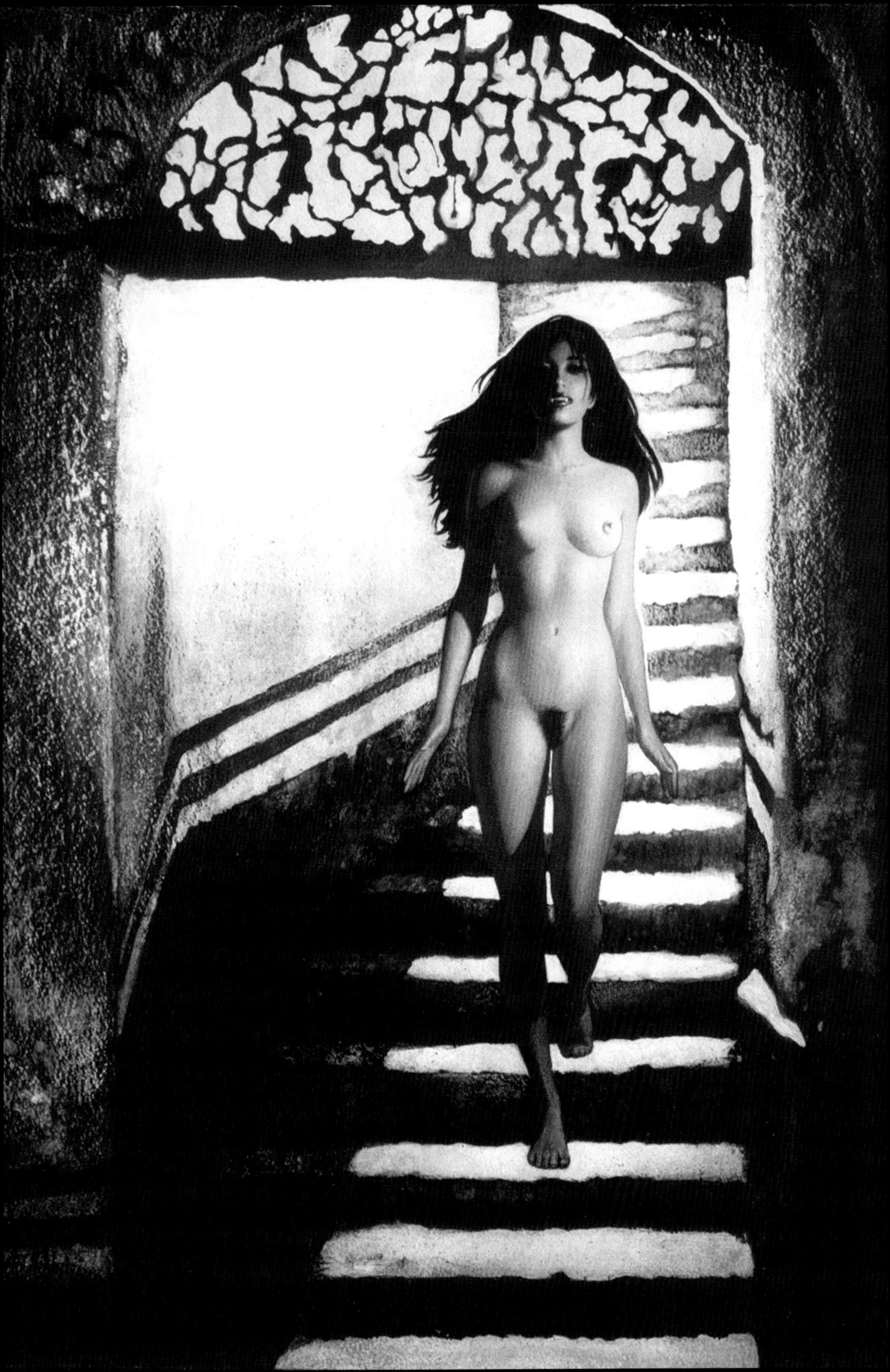

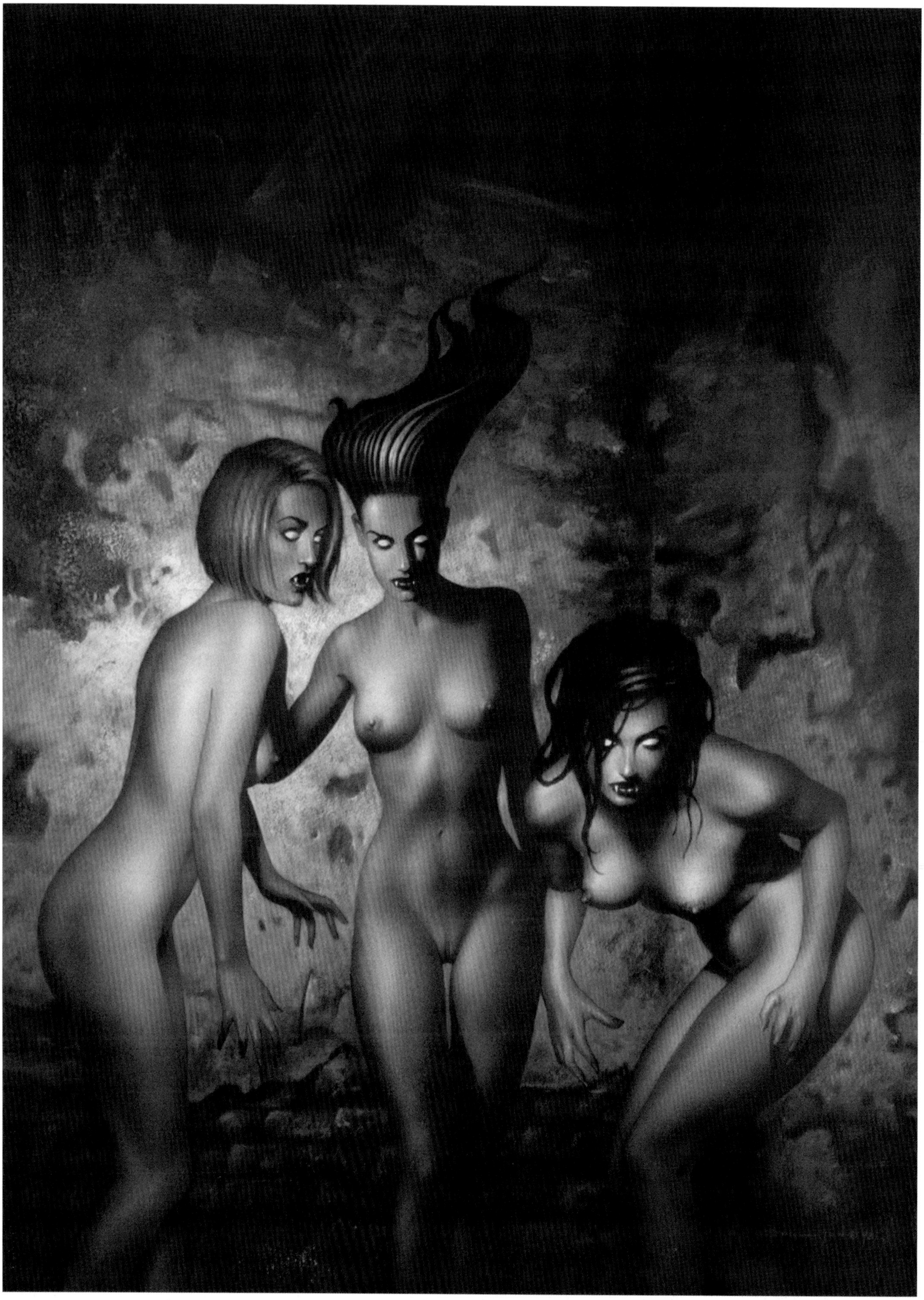

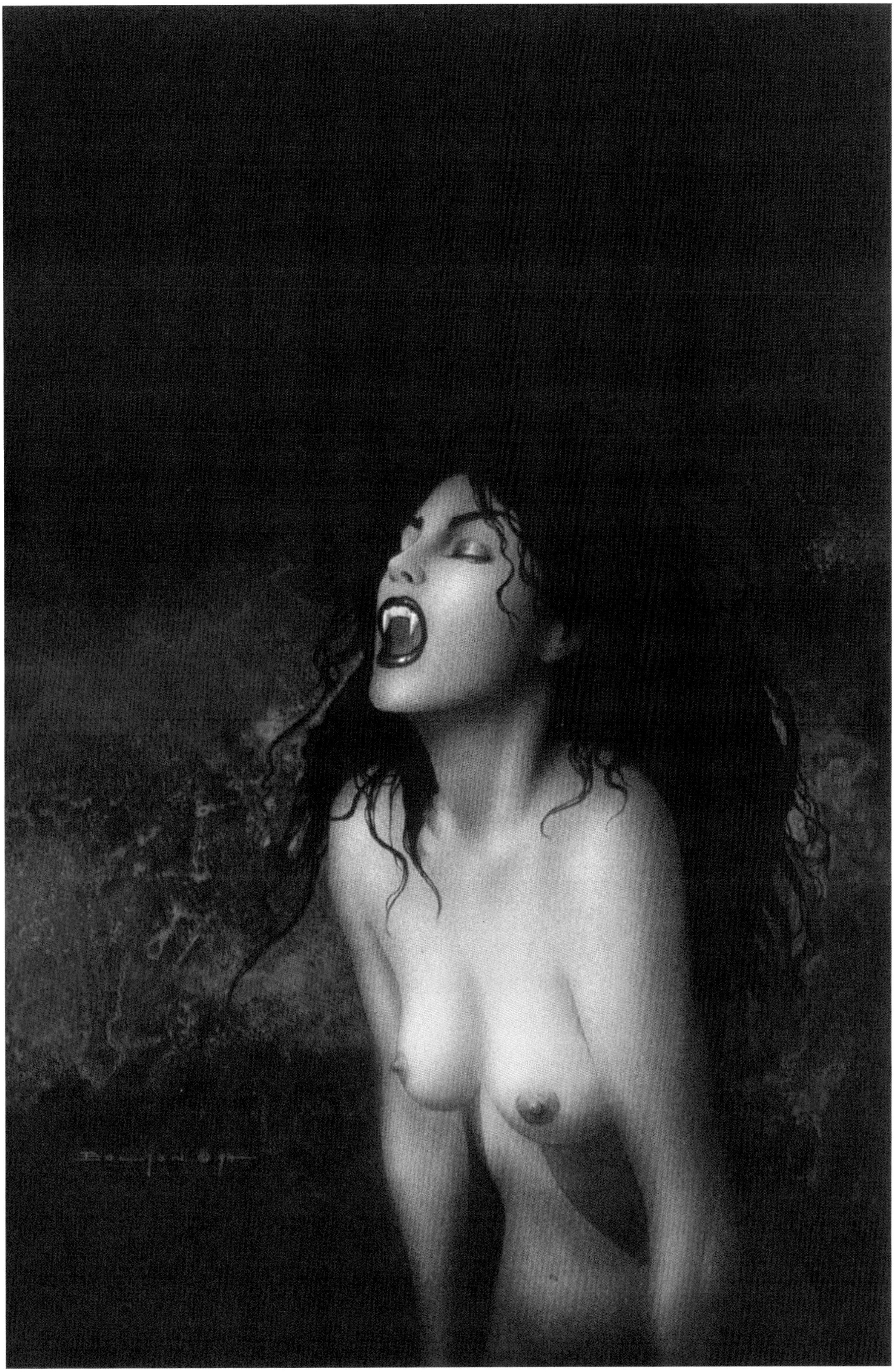

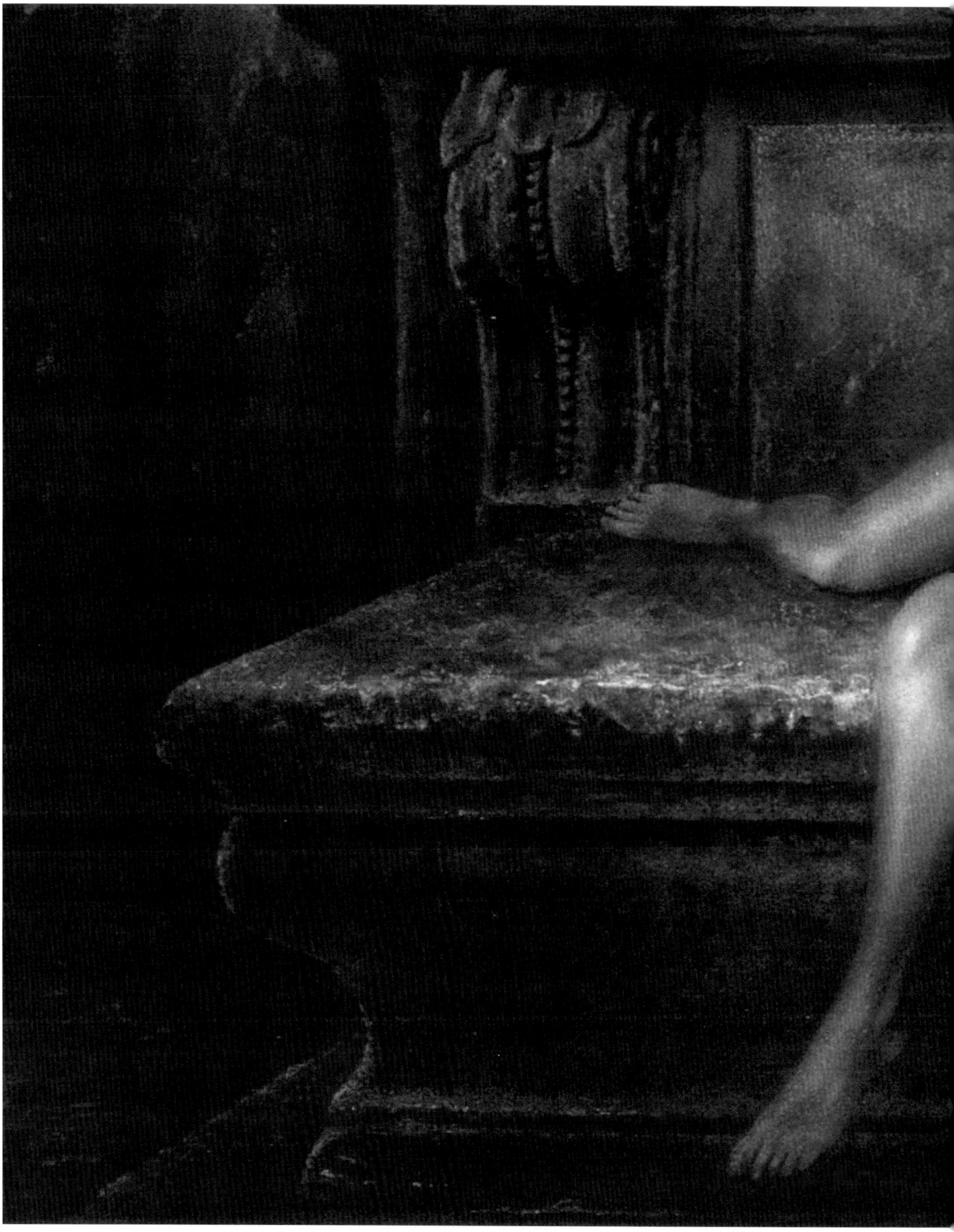

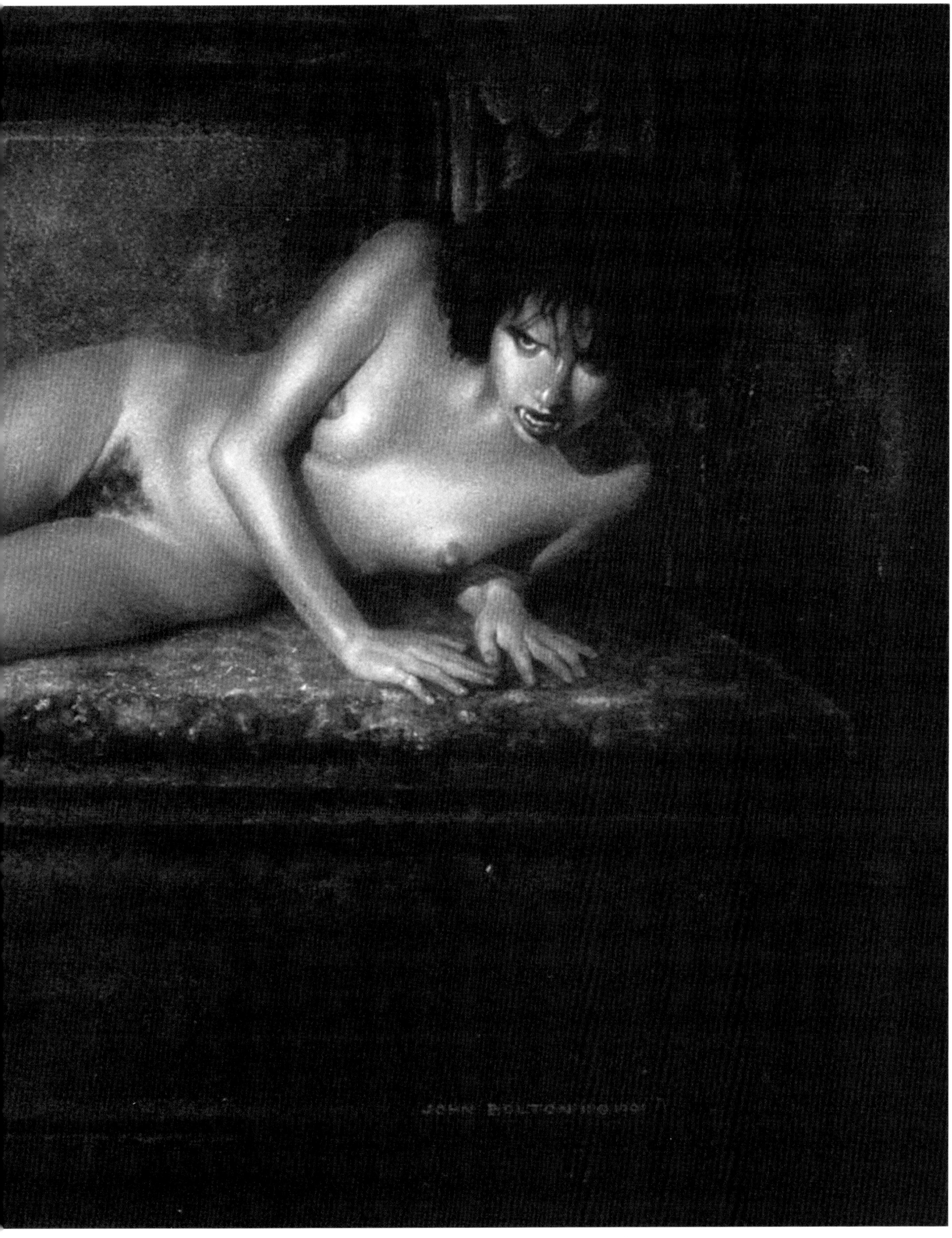
JOHN BOLTON

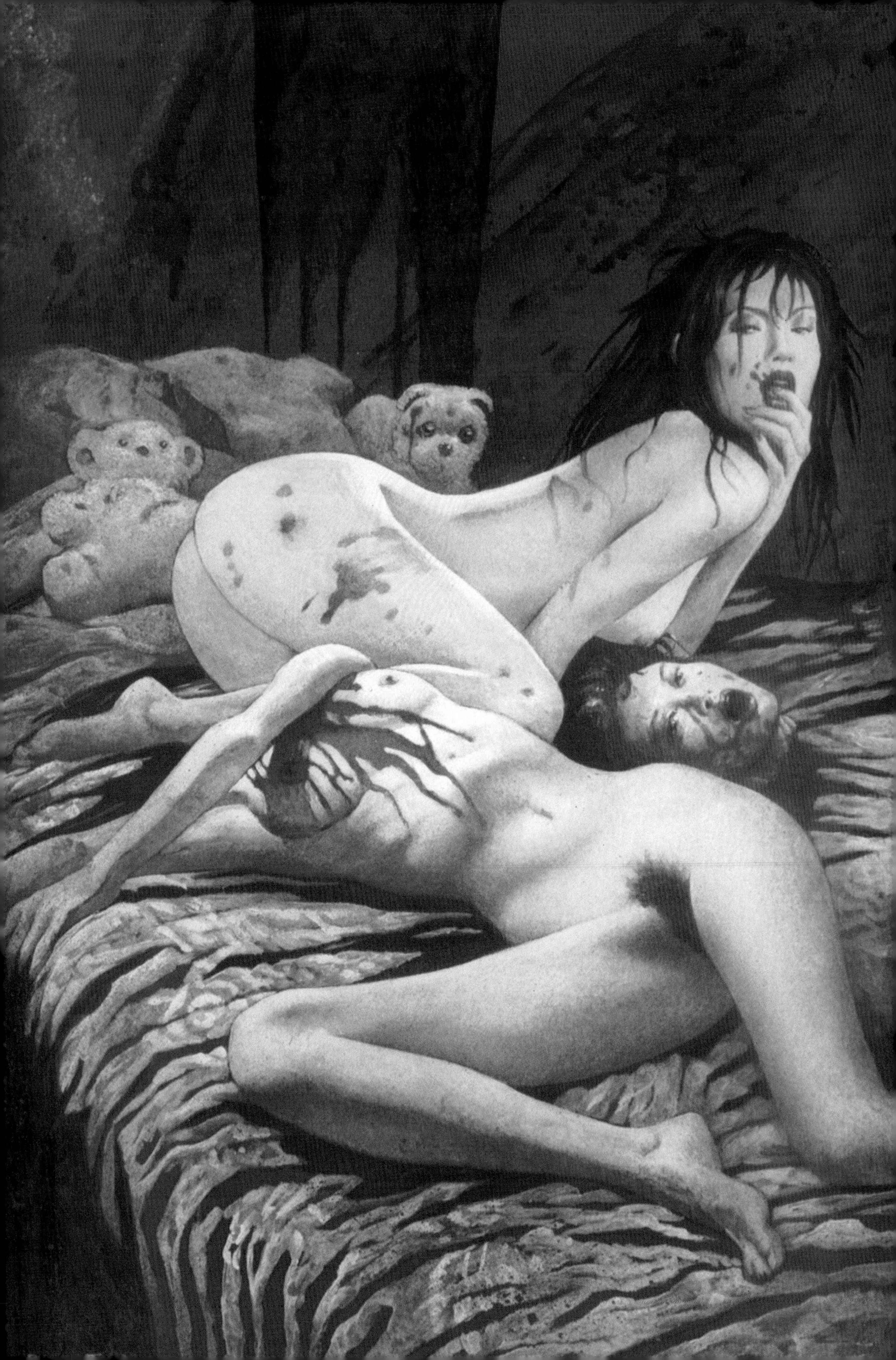

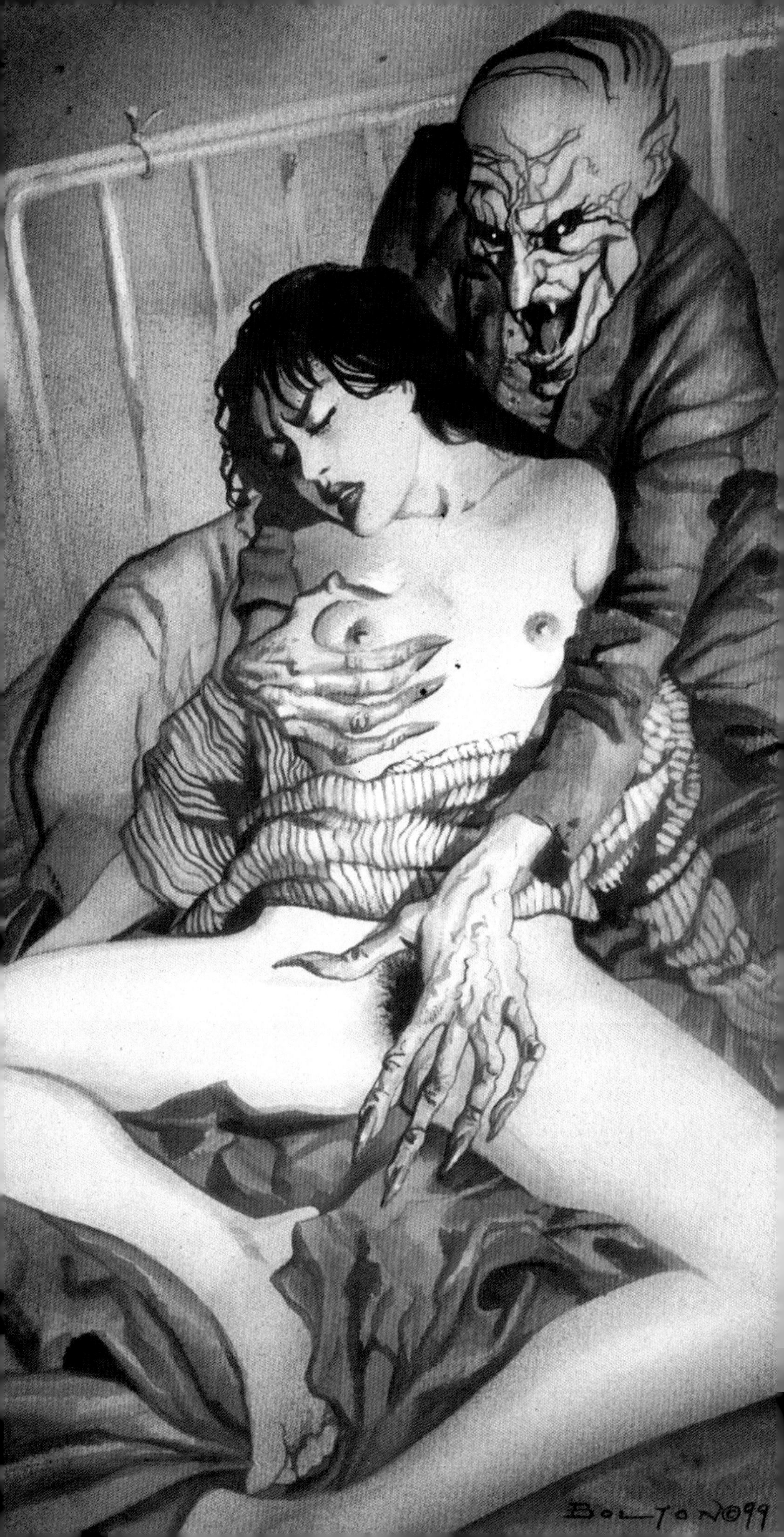
BOLTON©99

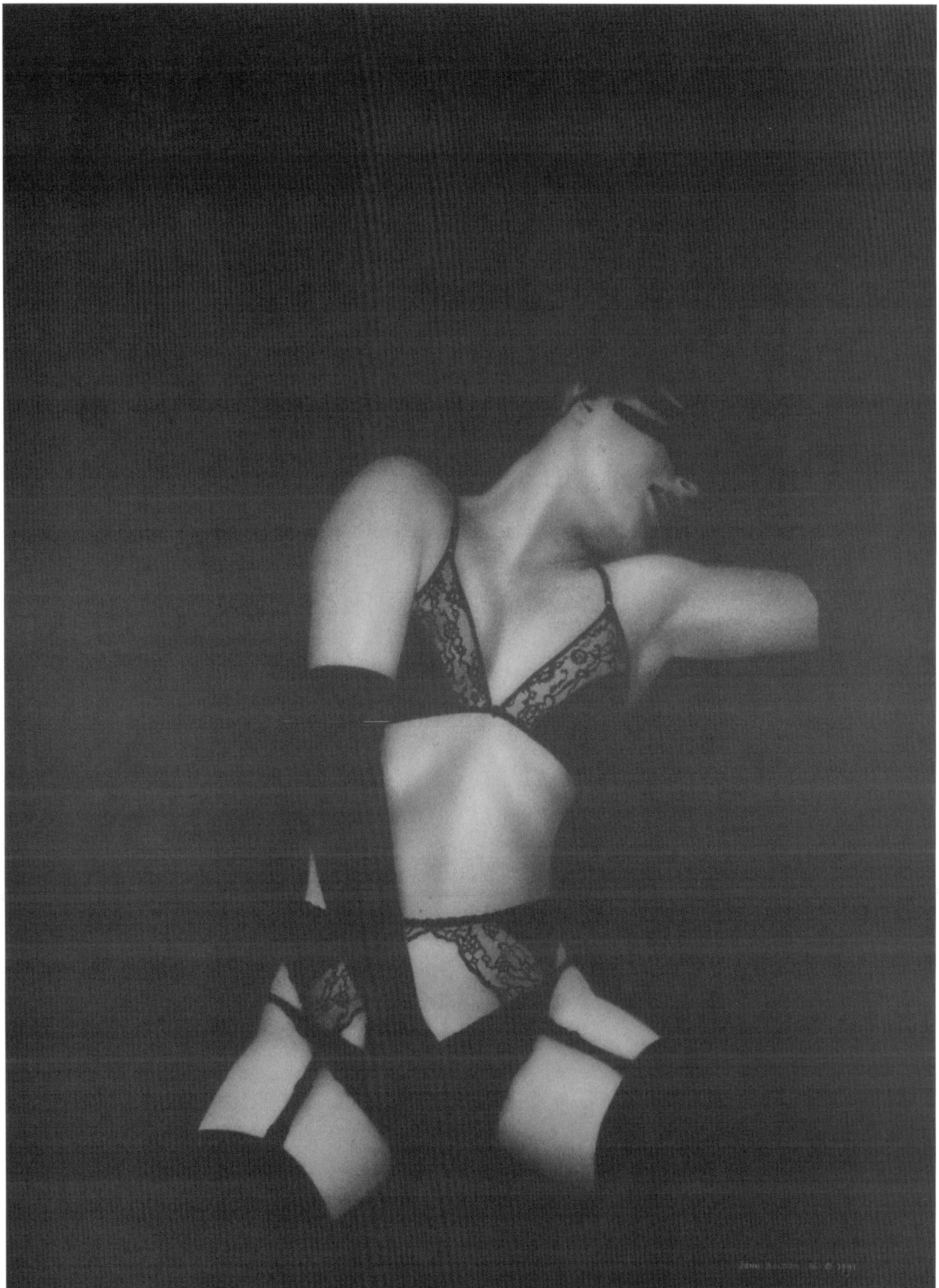

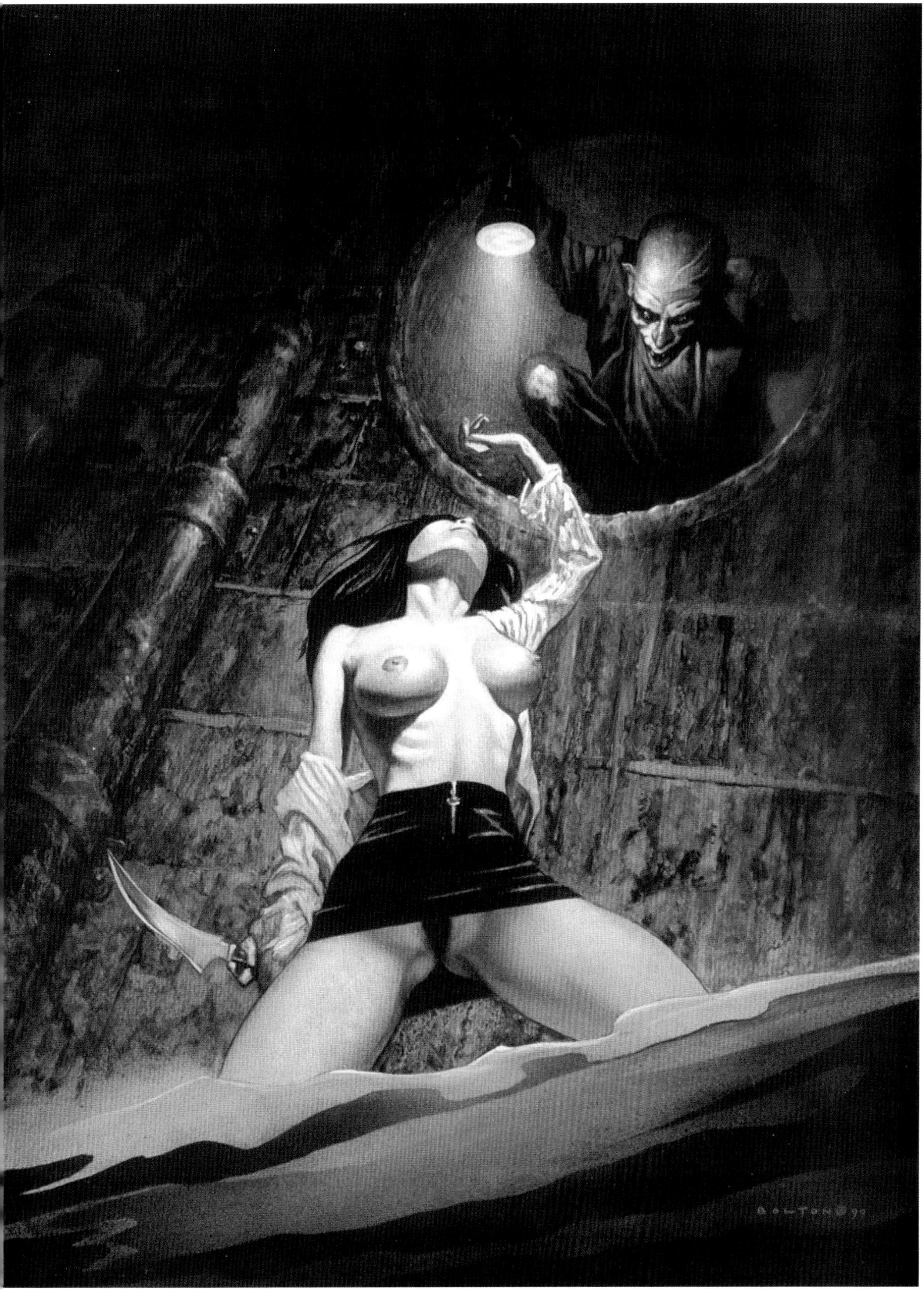
BOLTON©99

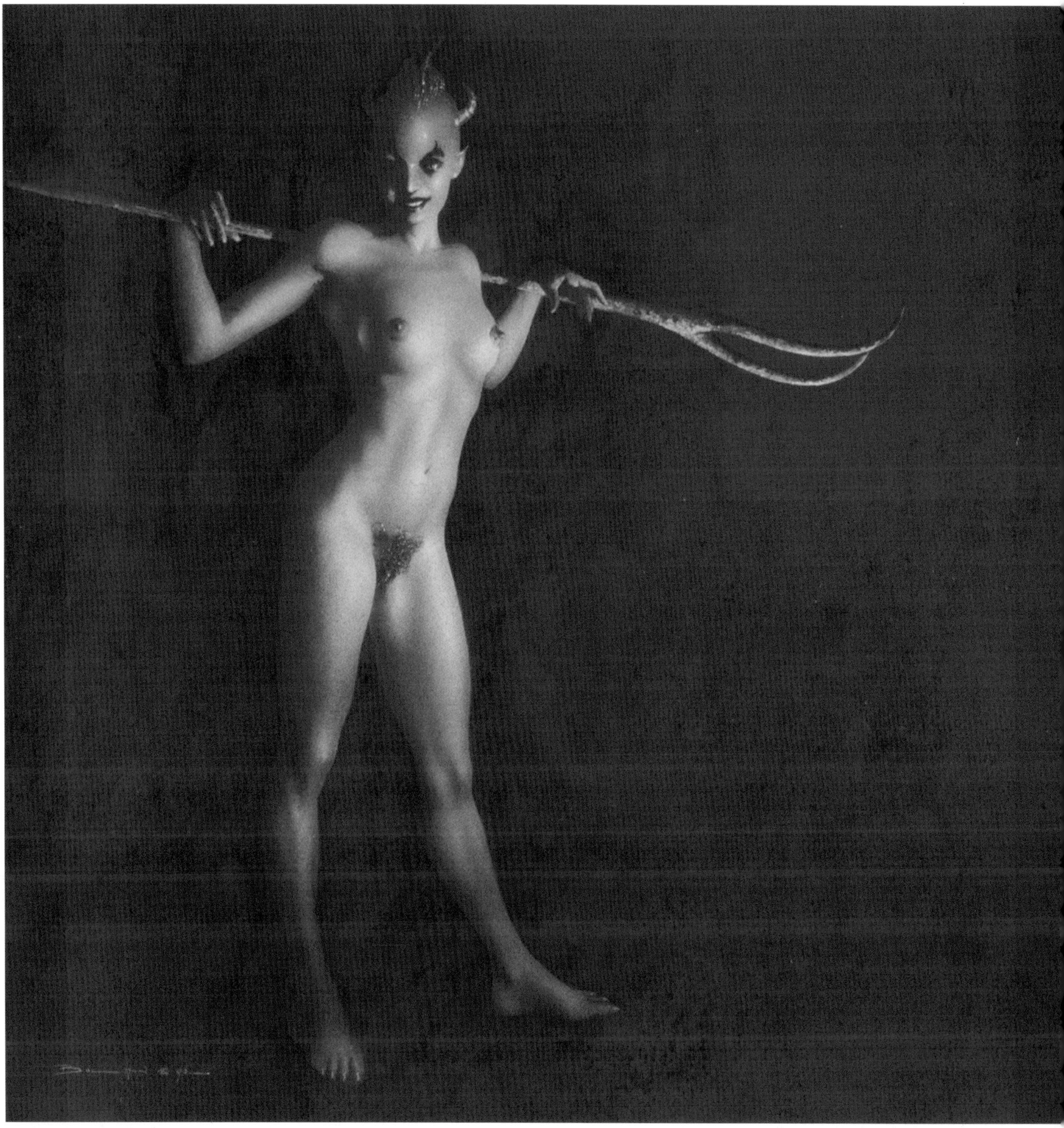

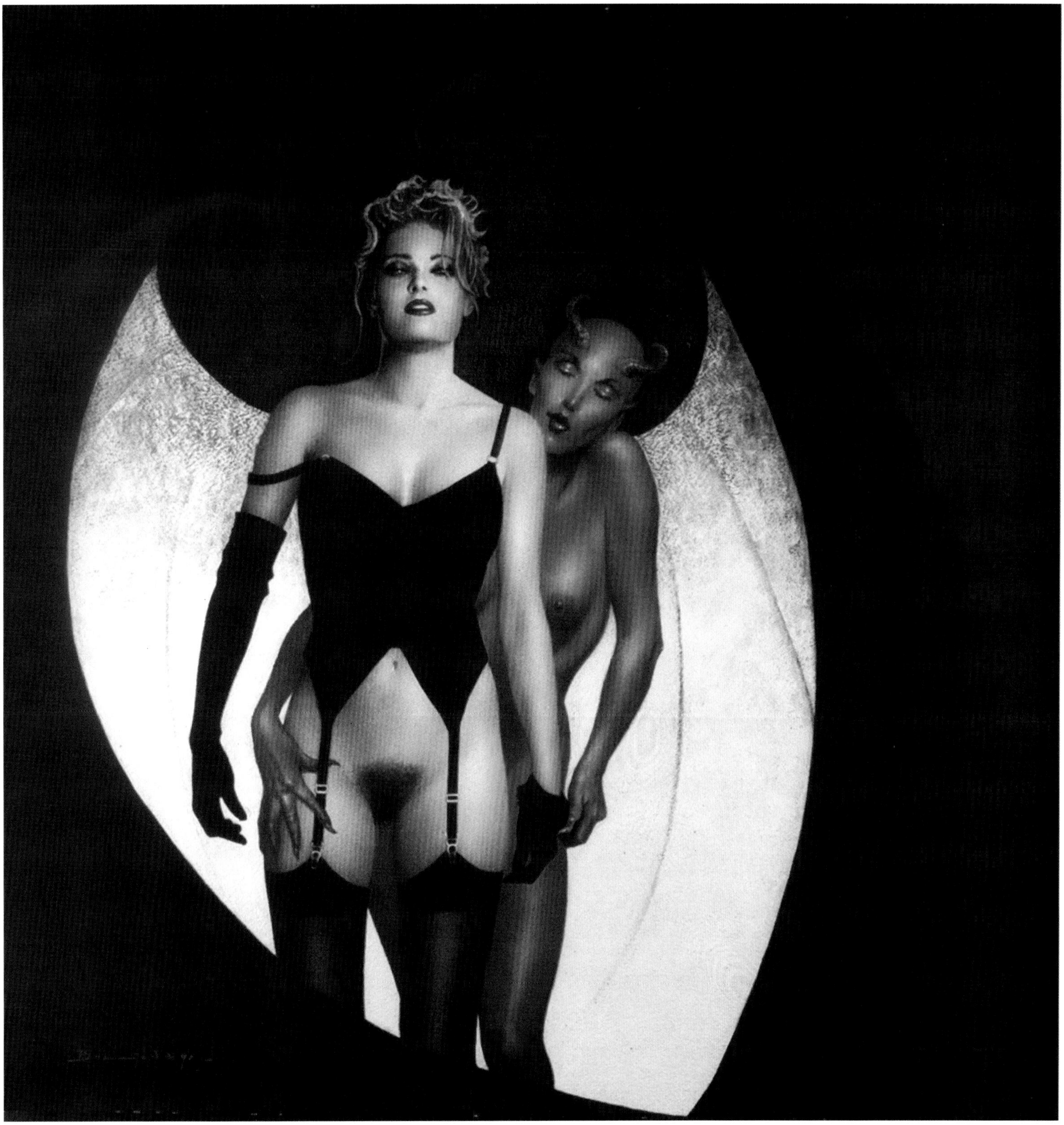

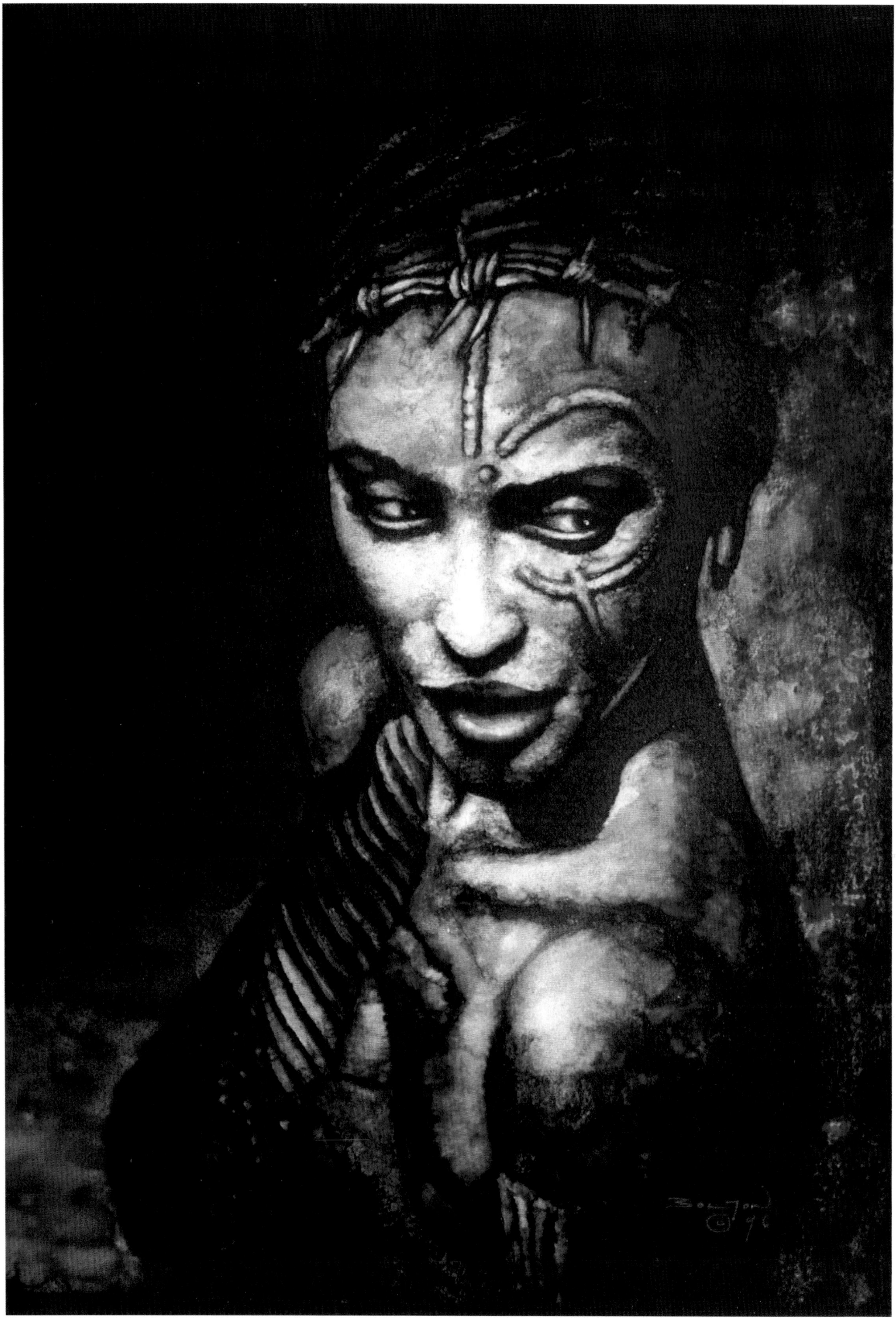

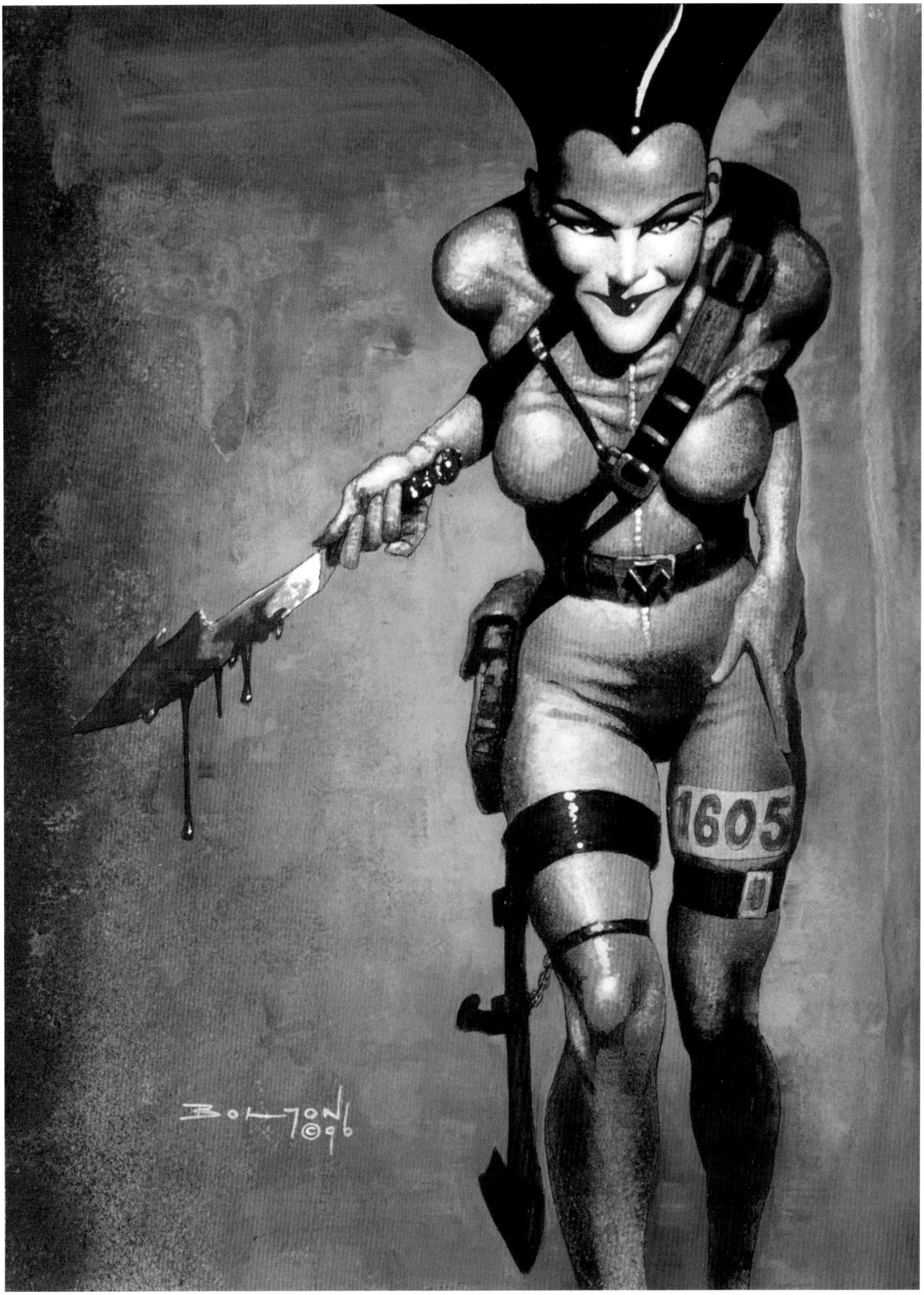
1605
BOLTON ©96

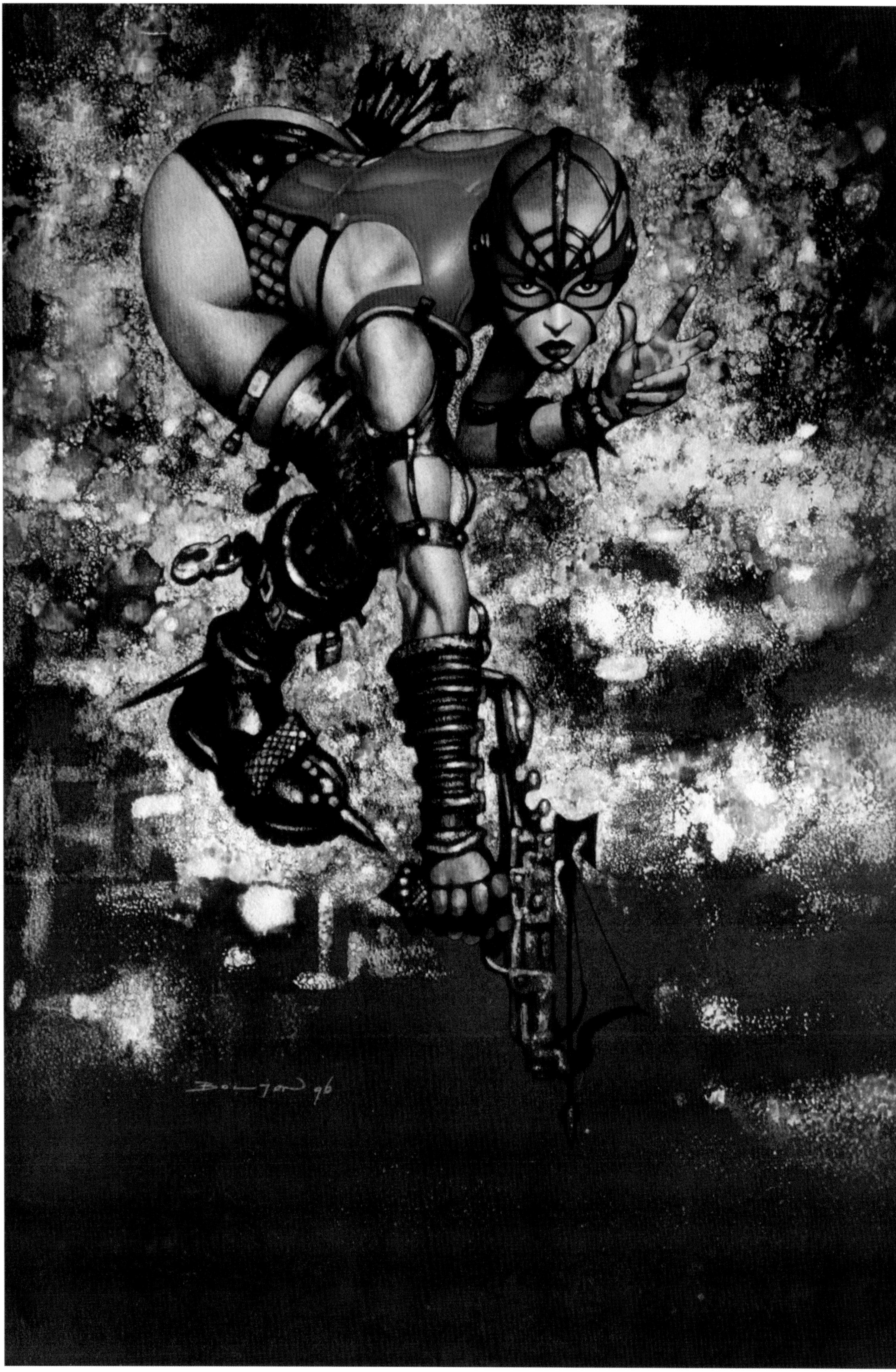
BOLTON 96

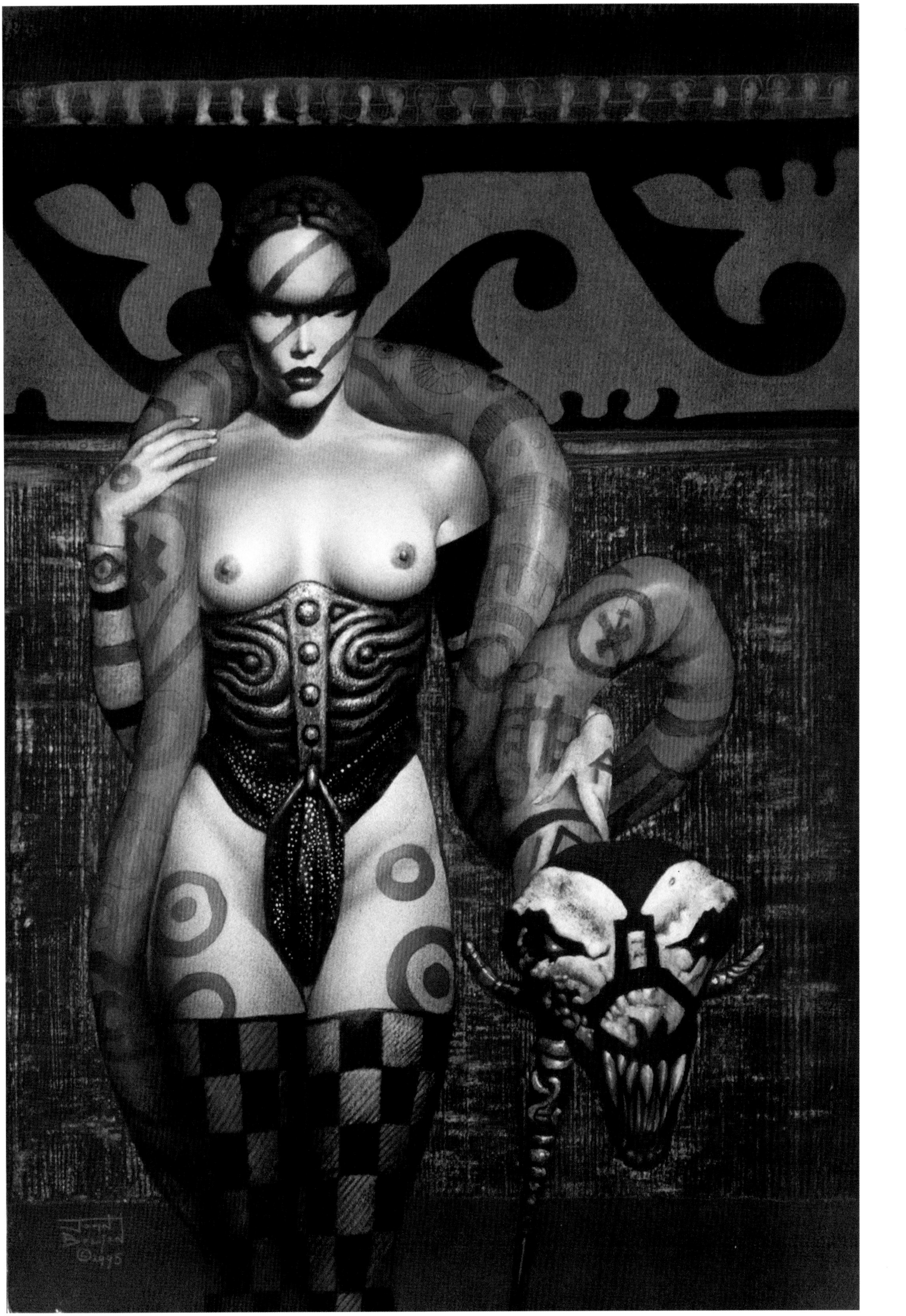

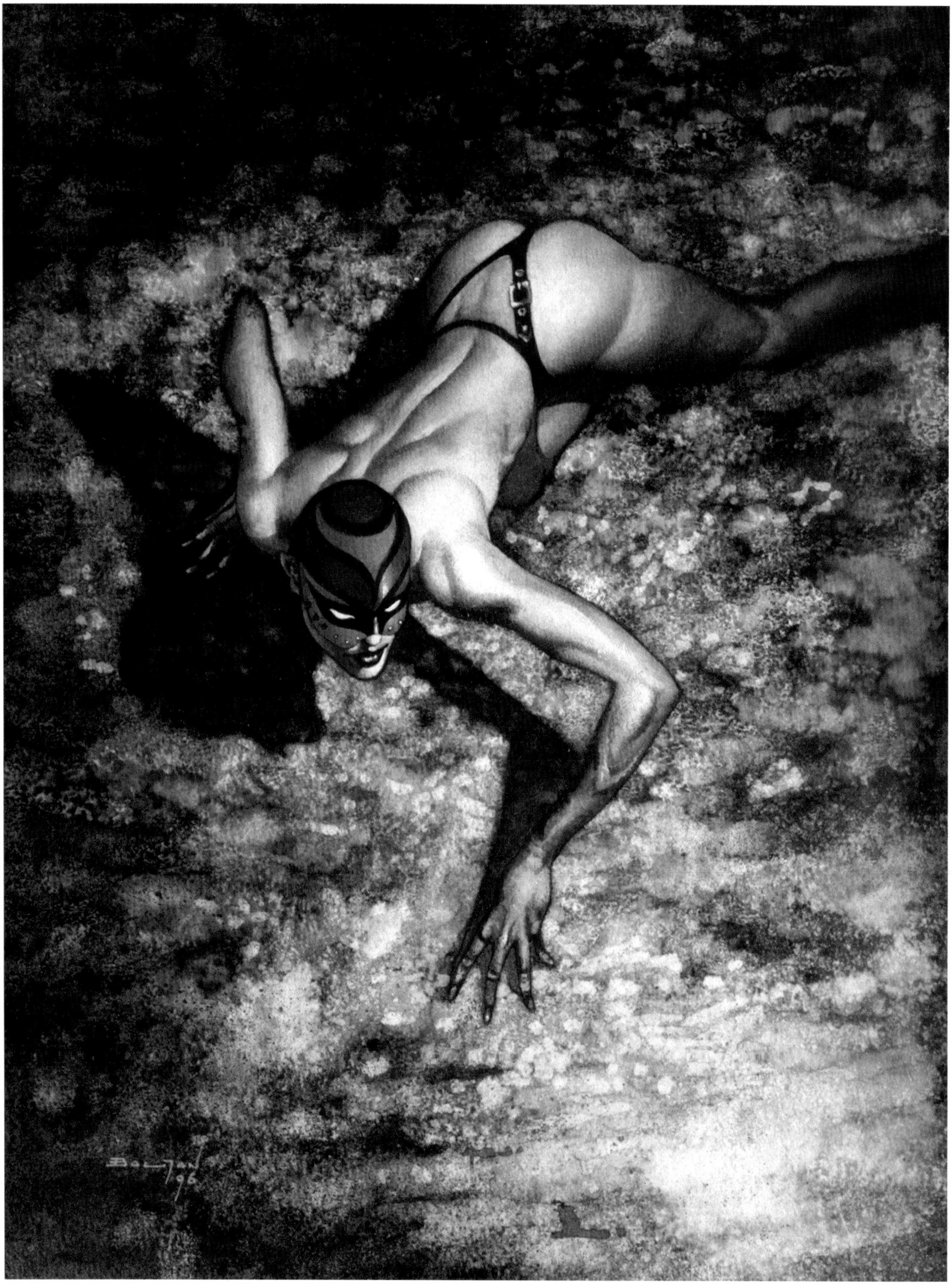

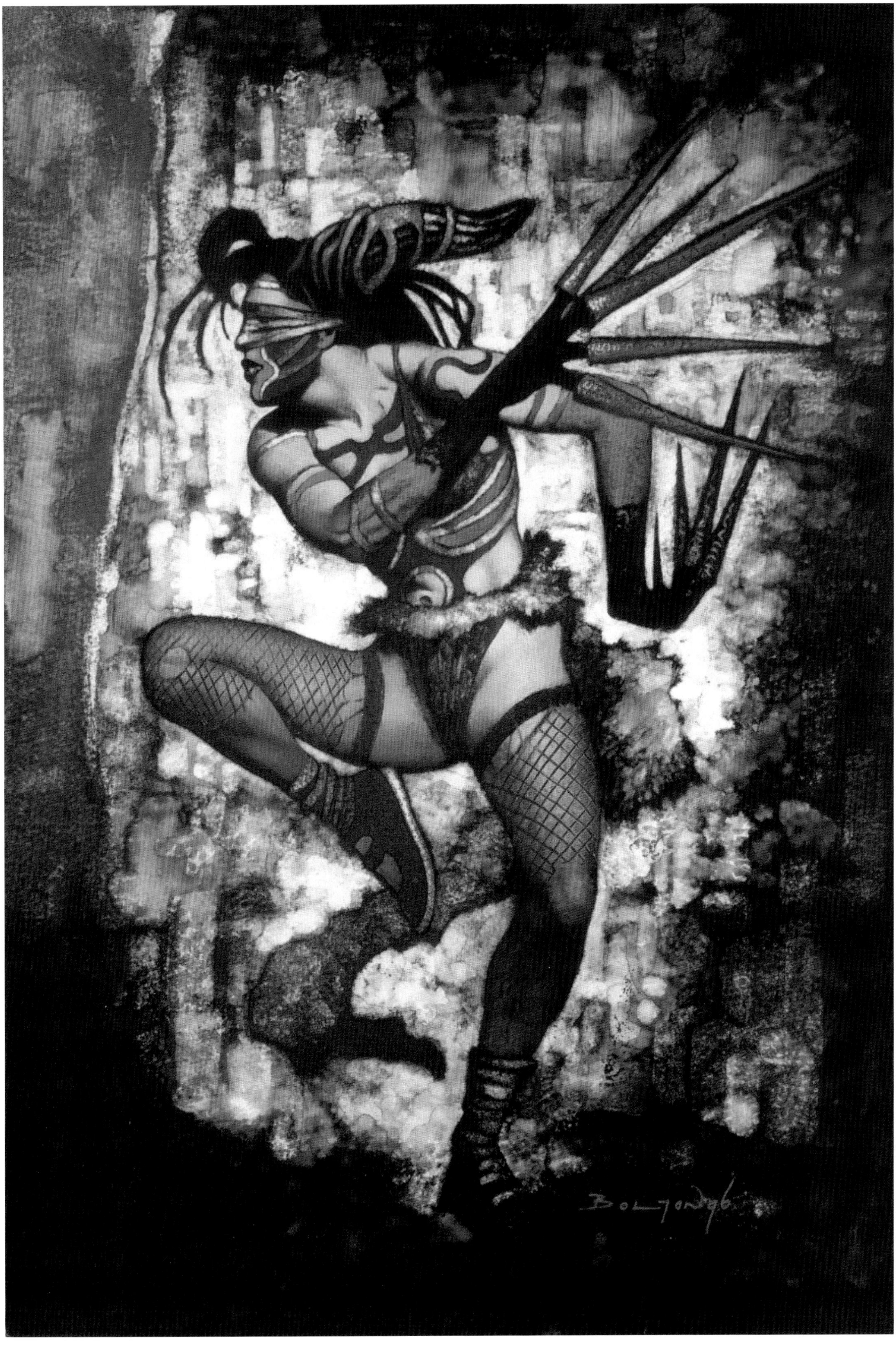
BOLTON 96

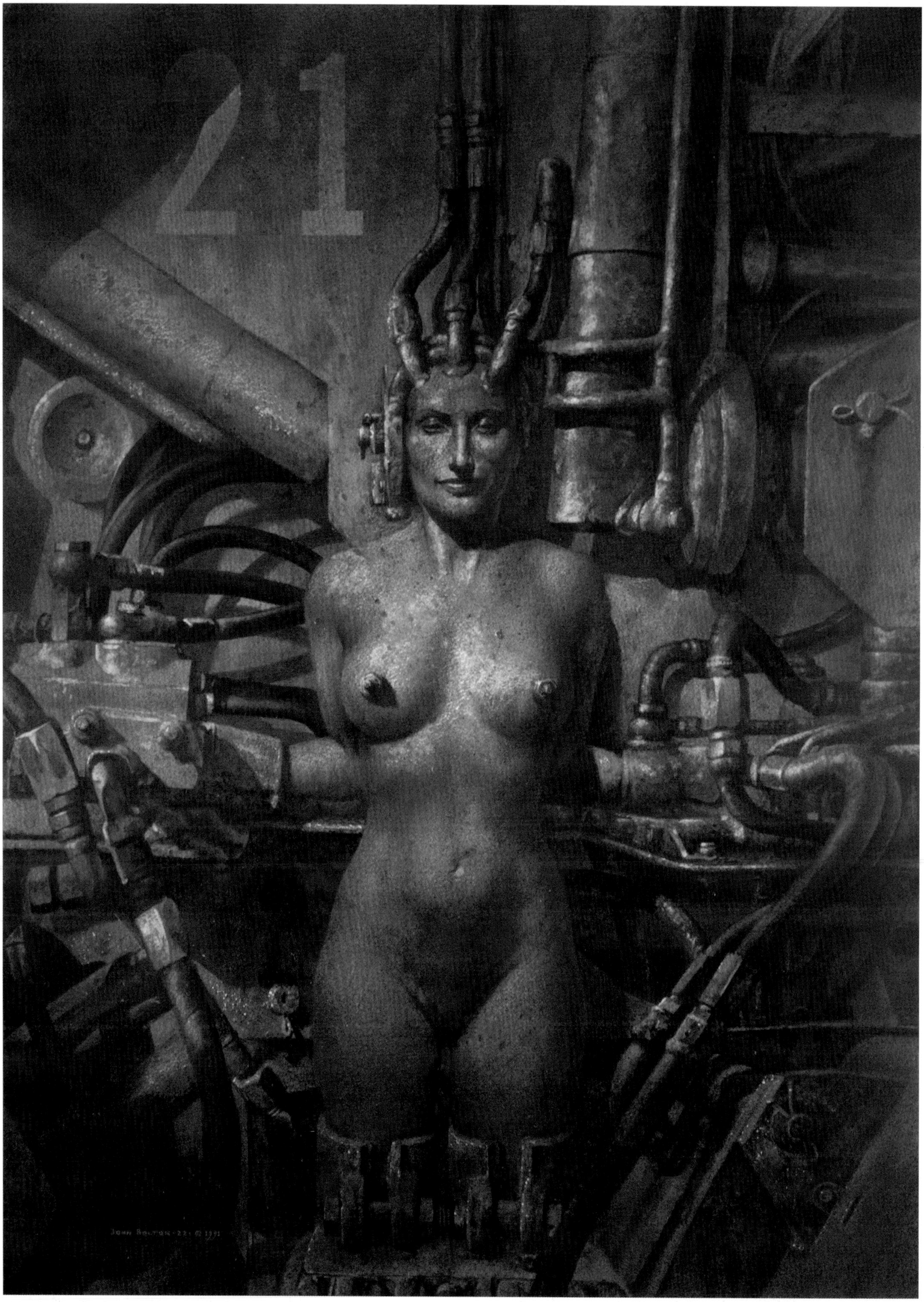

JOHN BOLTON · 22 · © 1991

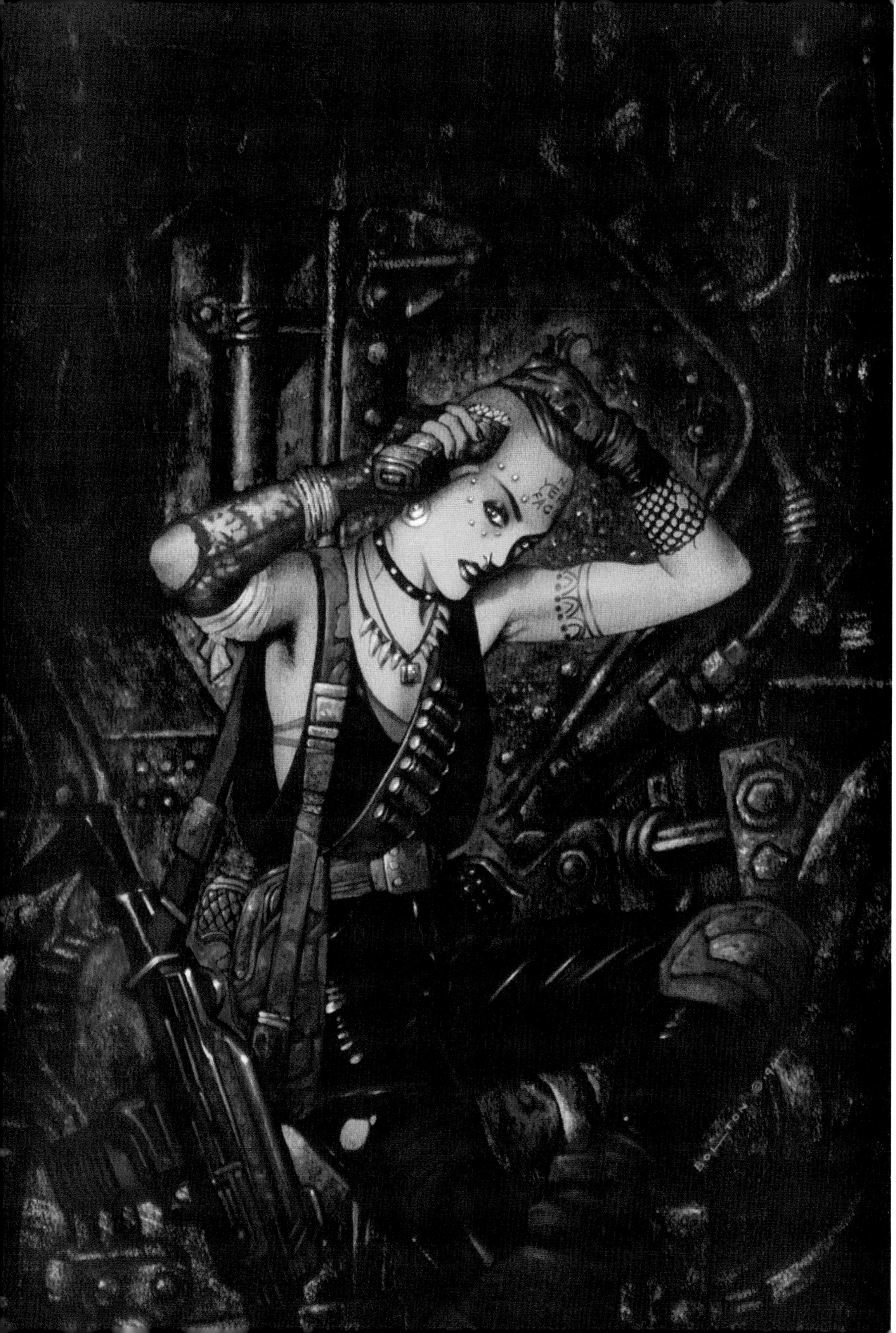

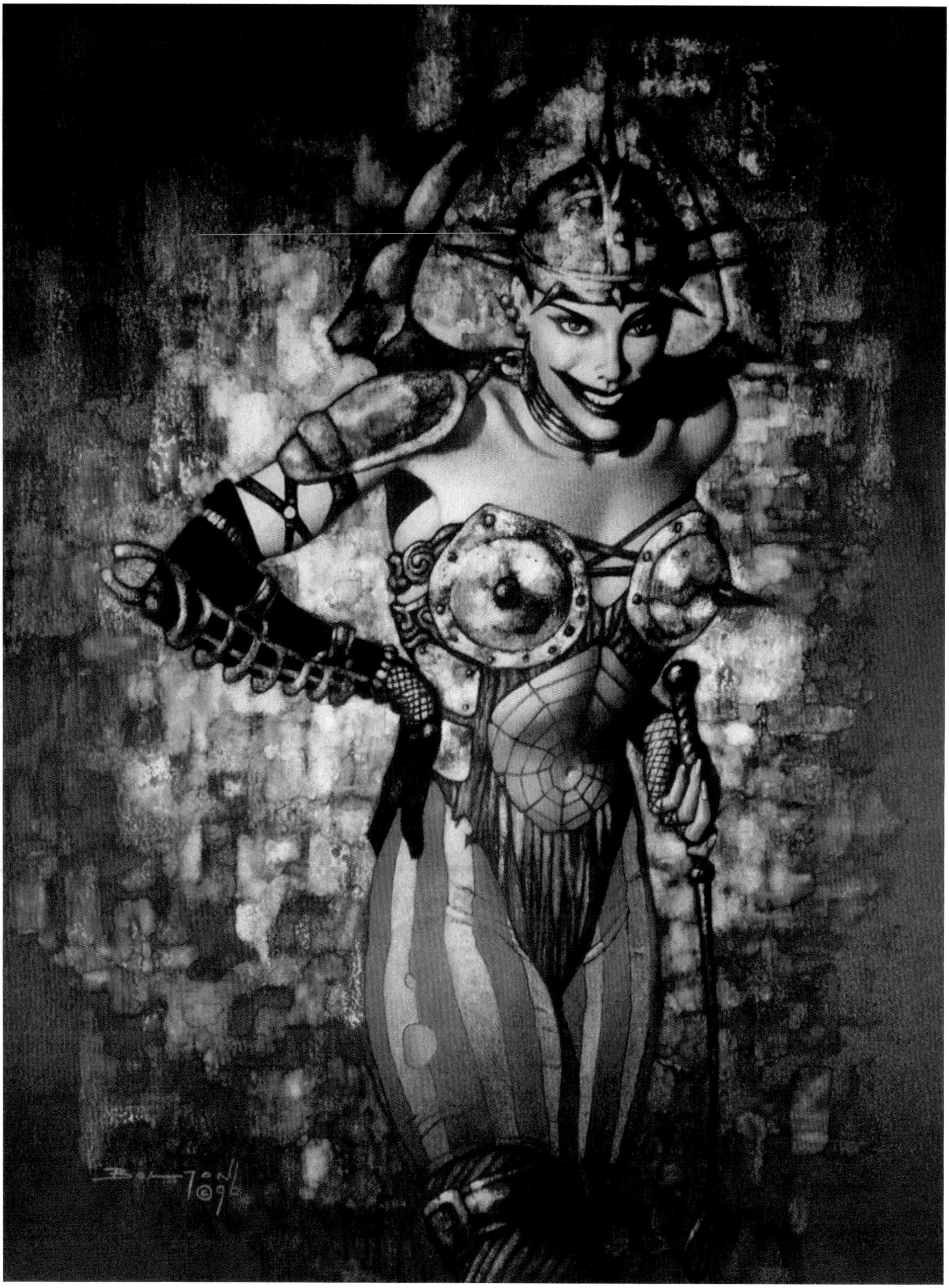

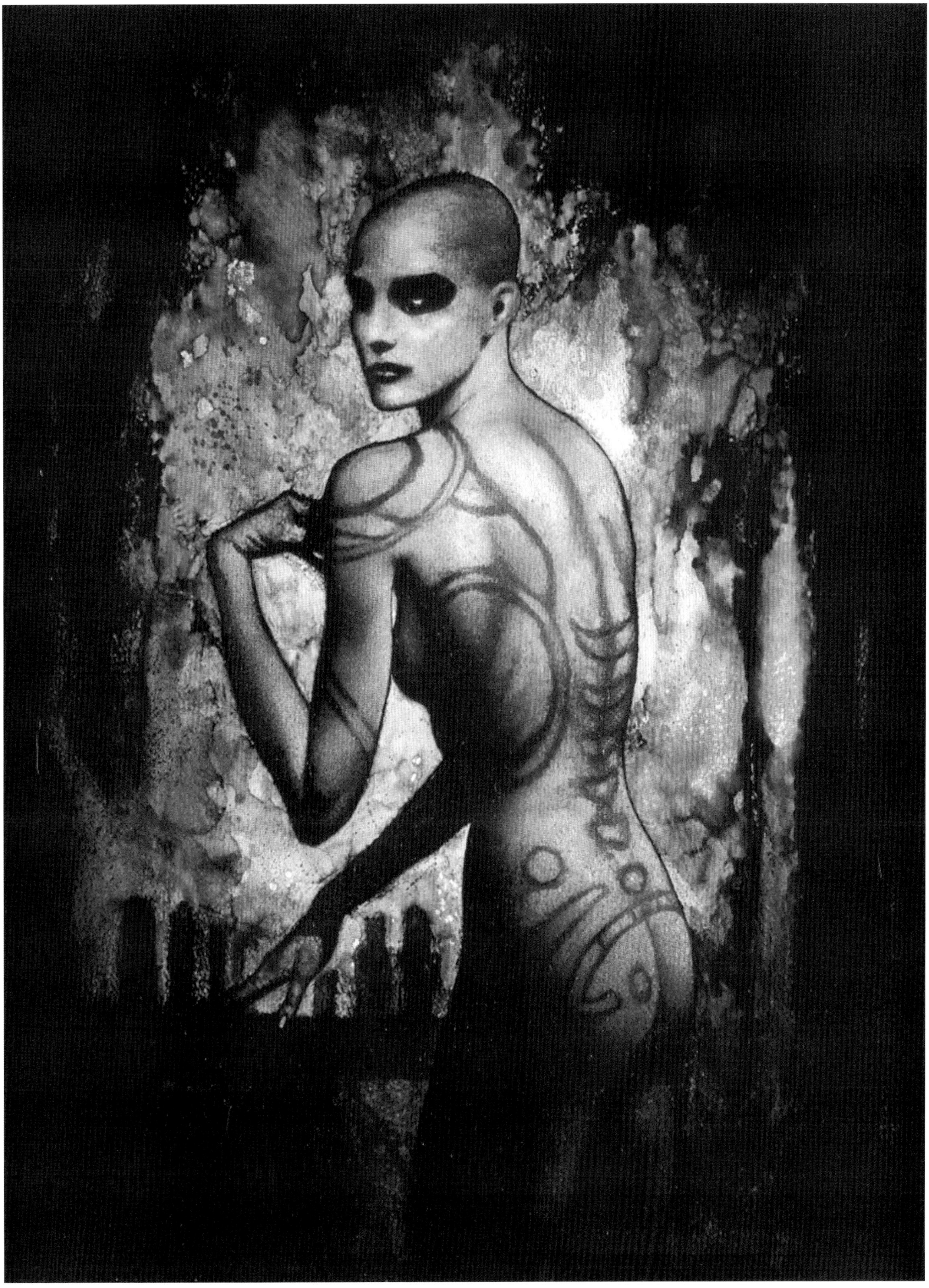

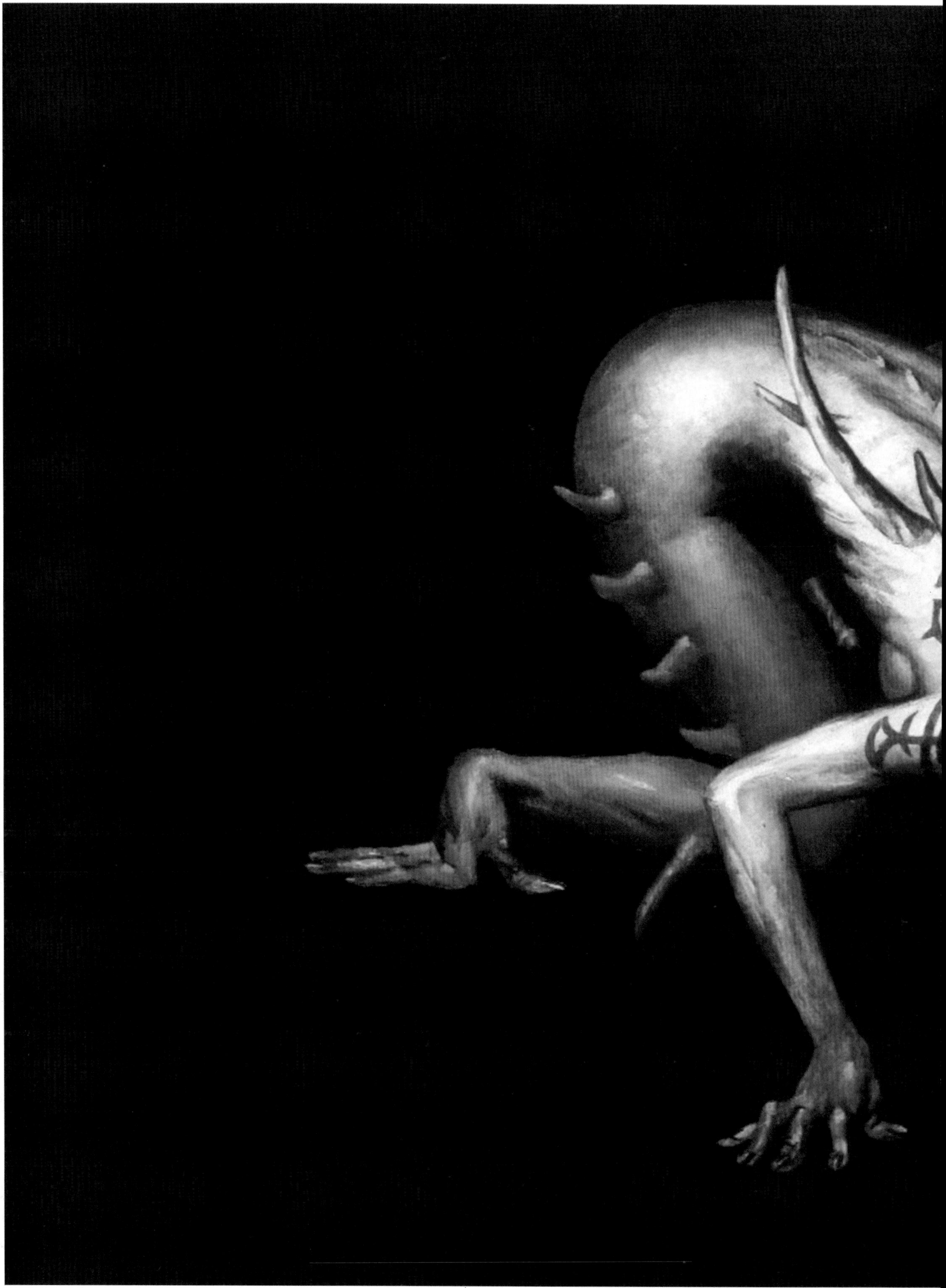

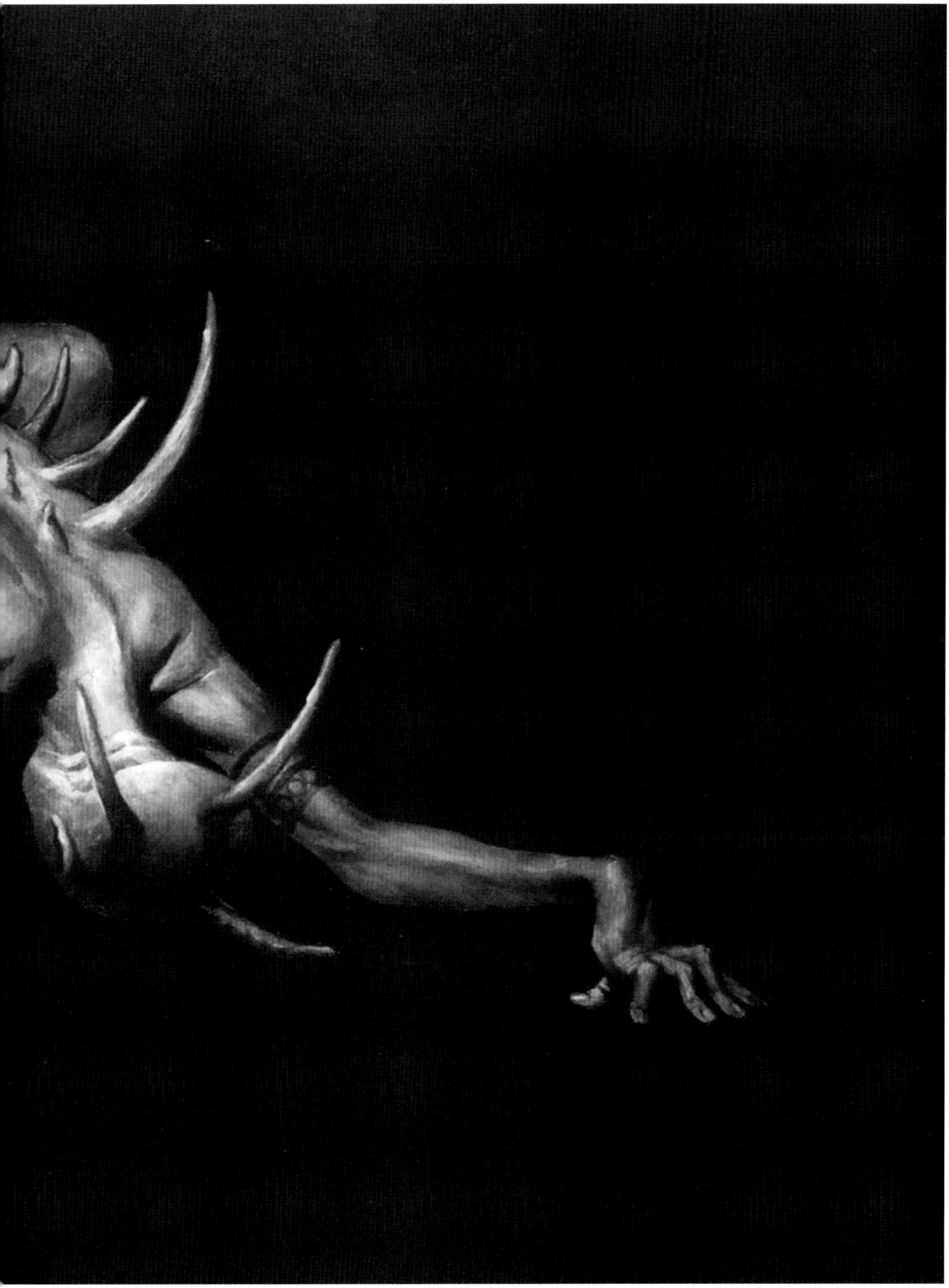

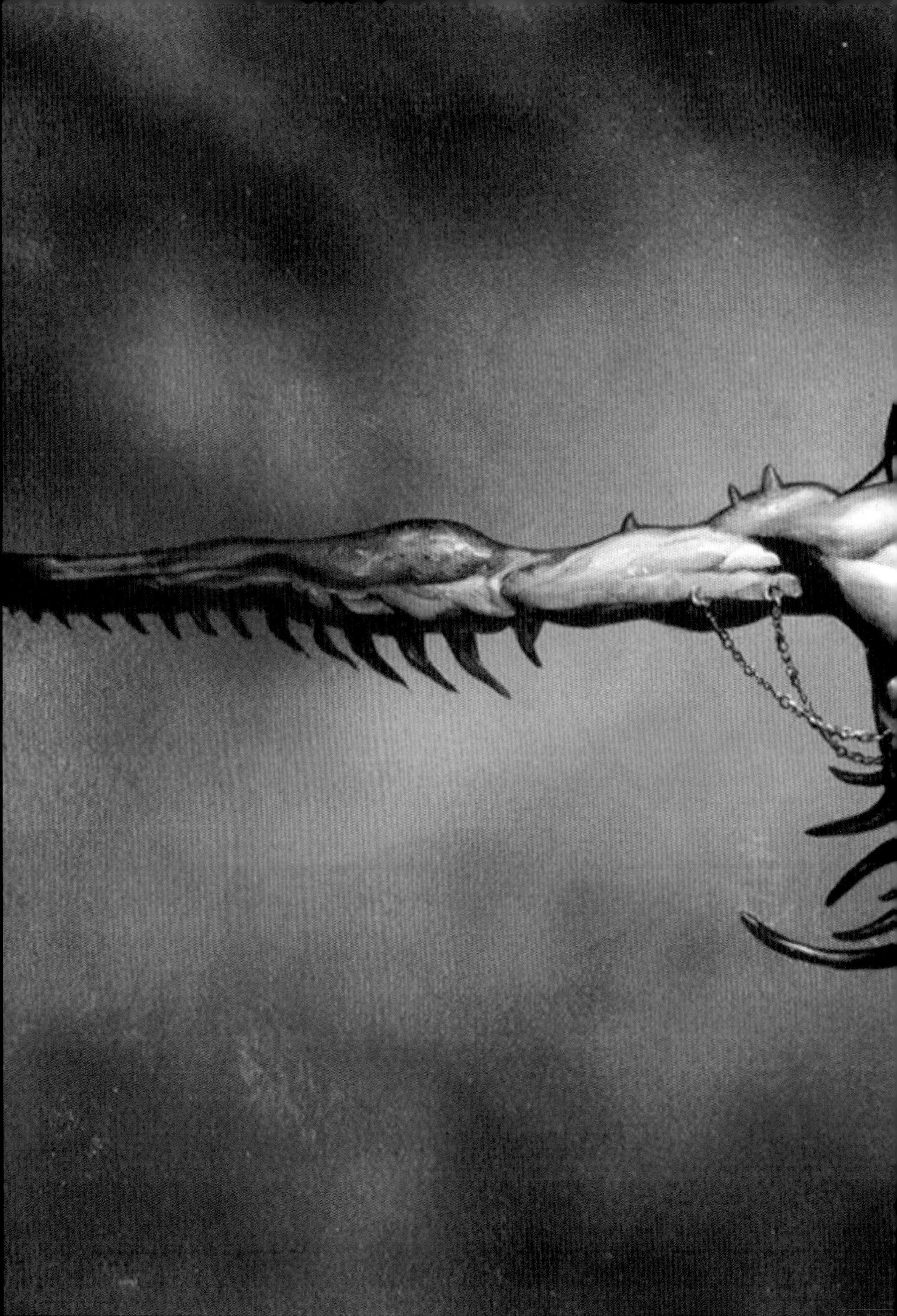

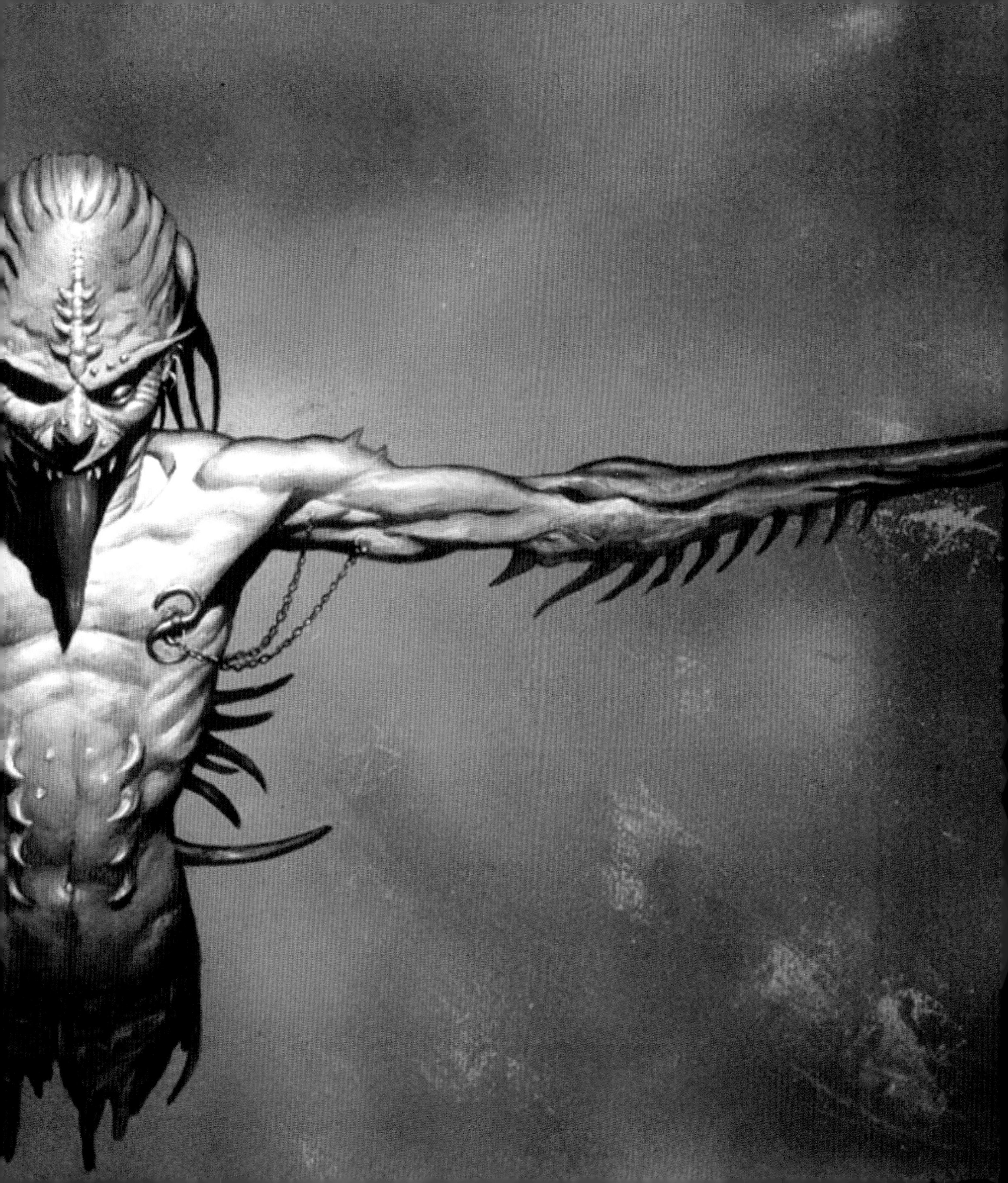

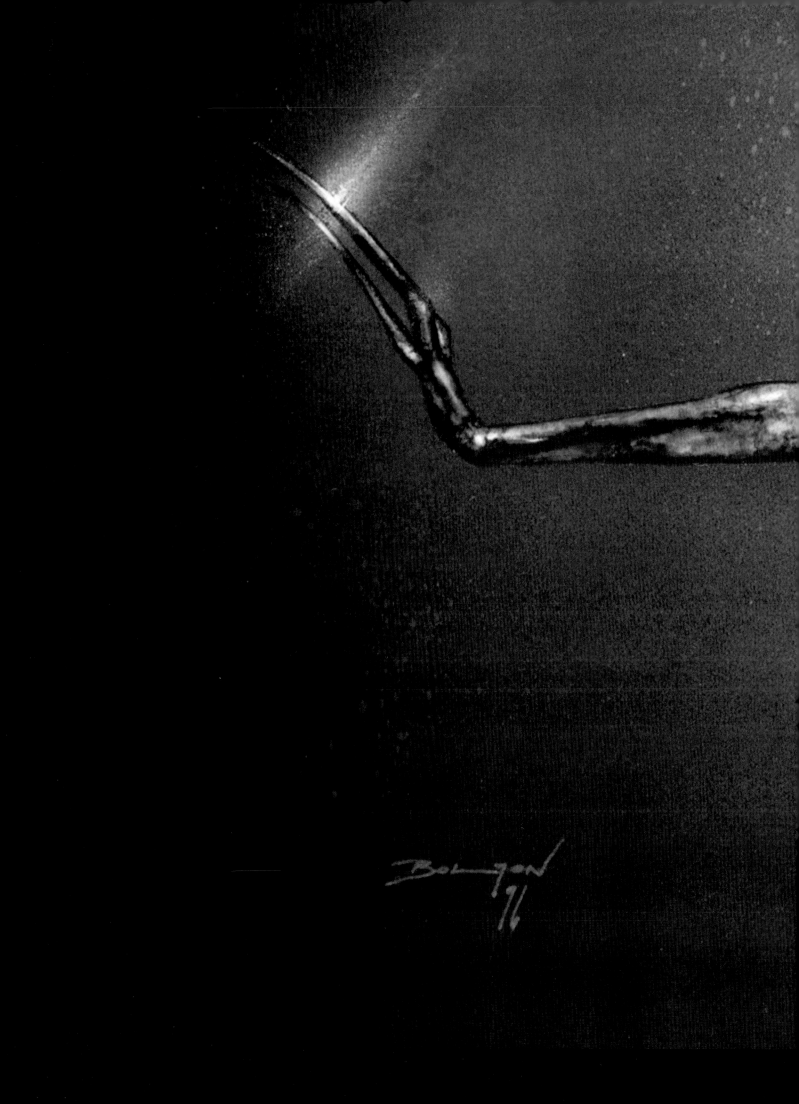

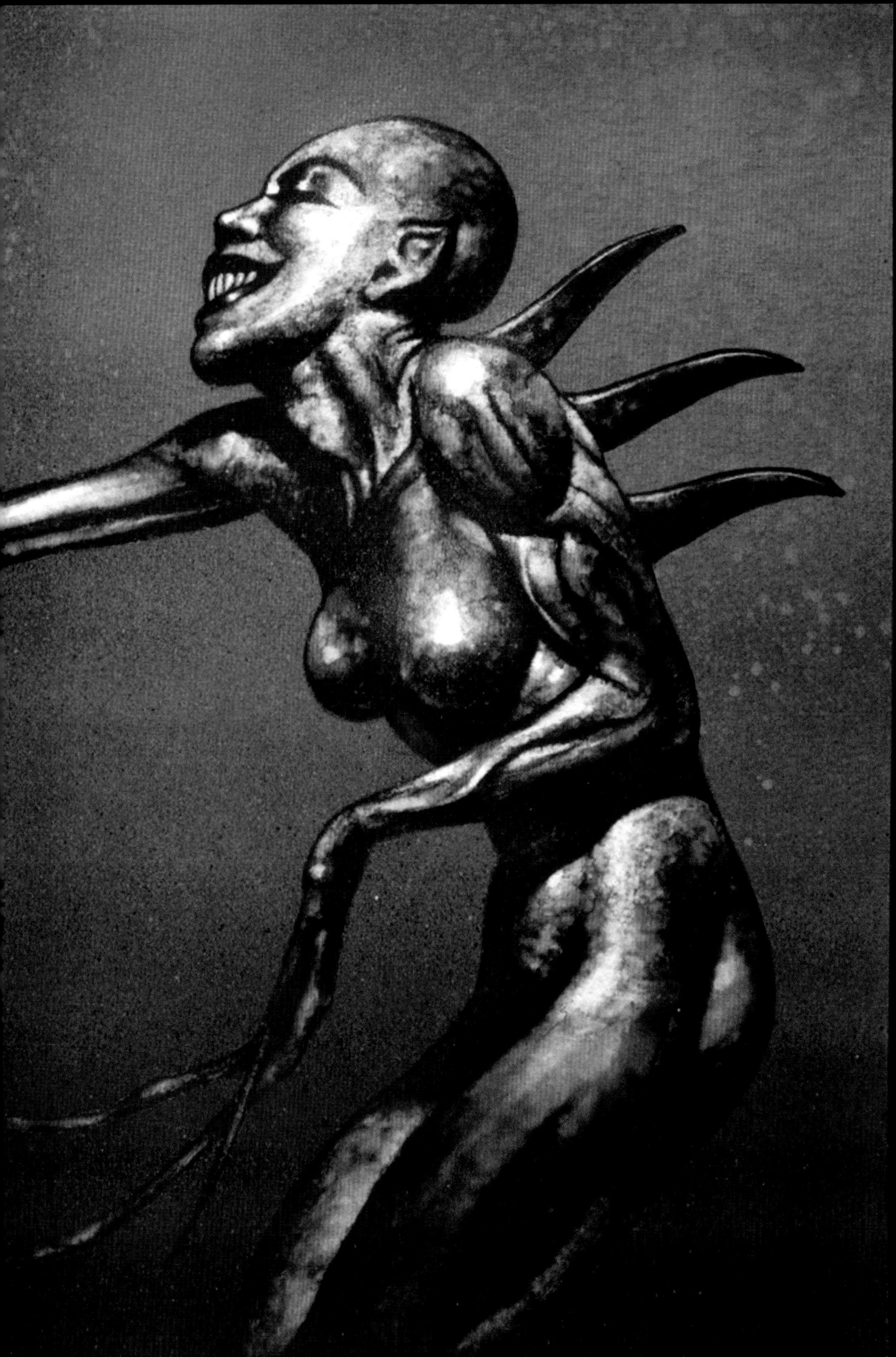

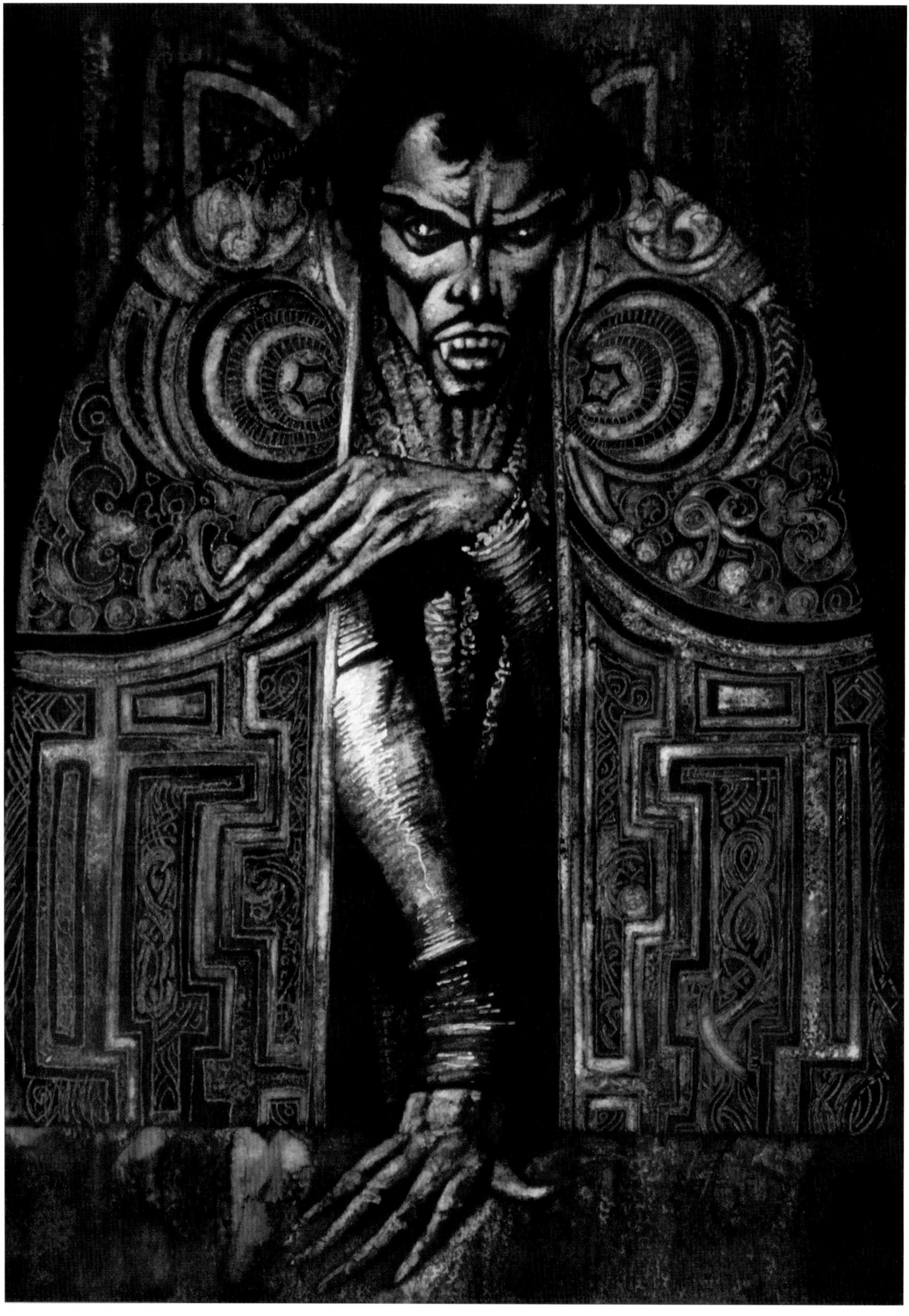

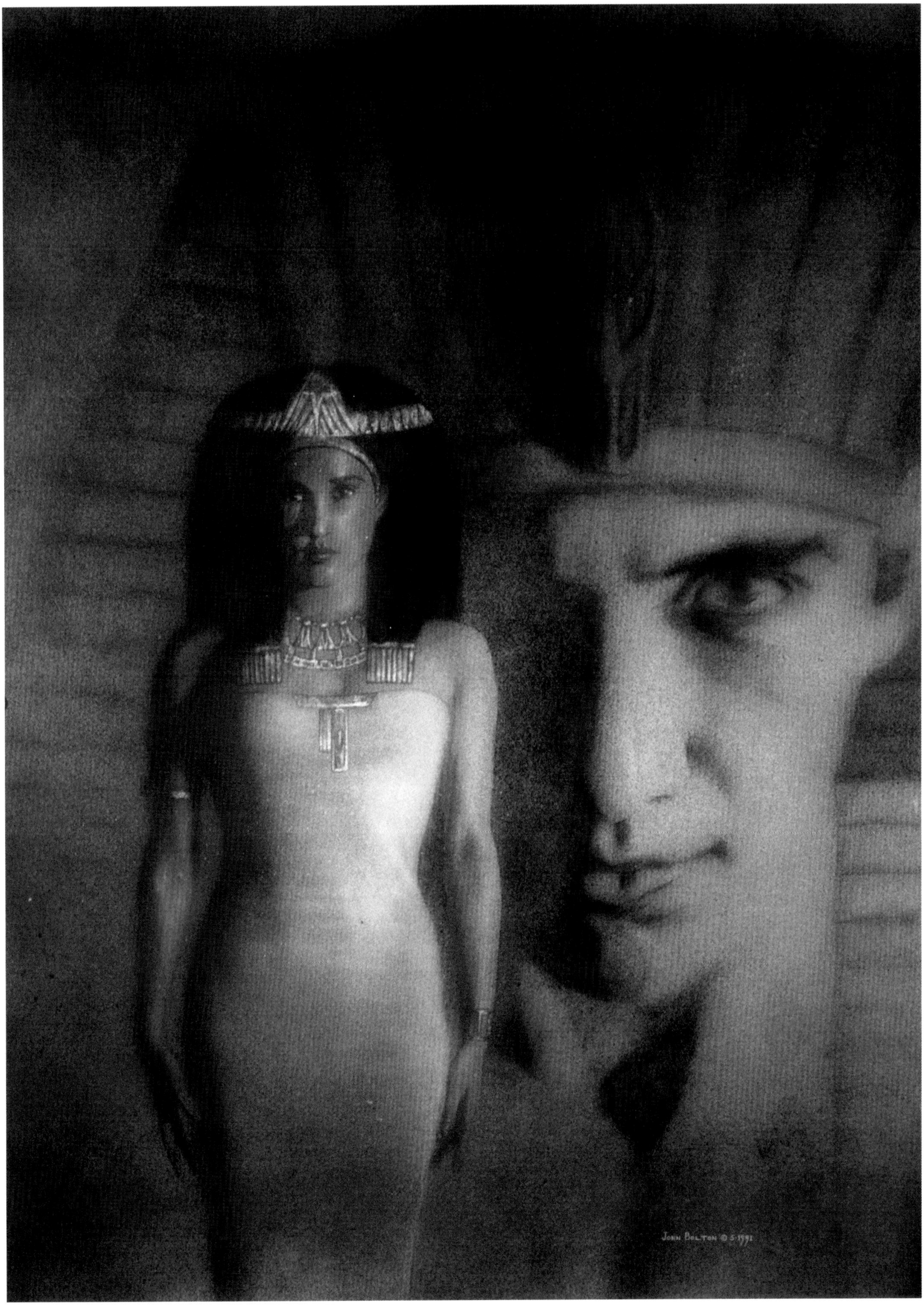
JOHN BOLTON © 5-1991

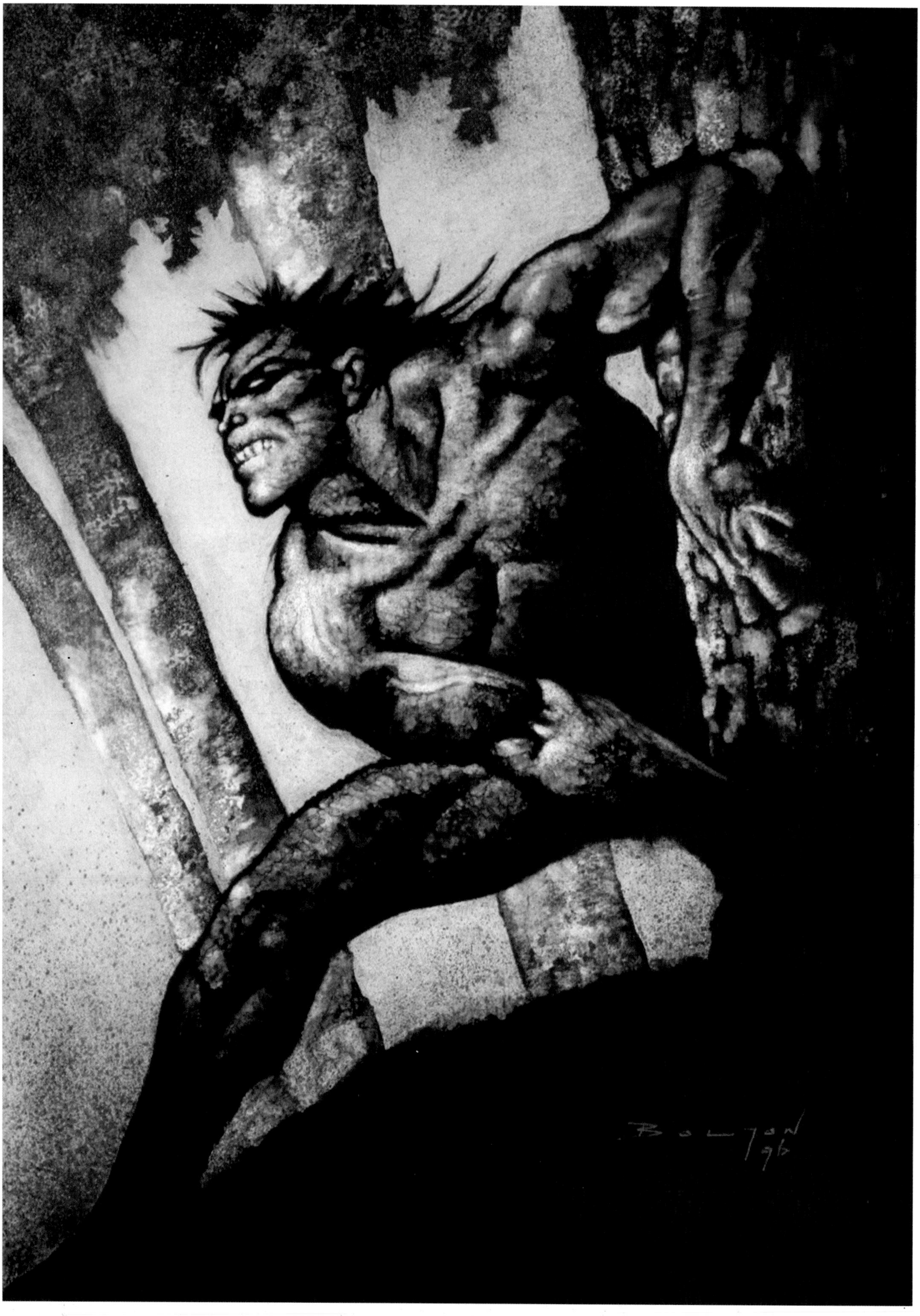

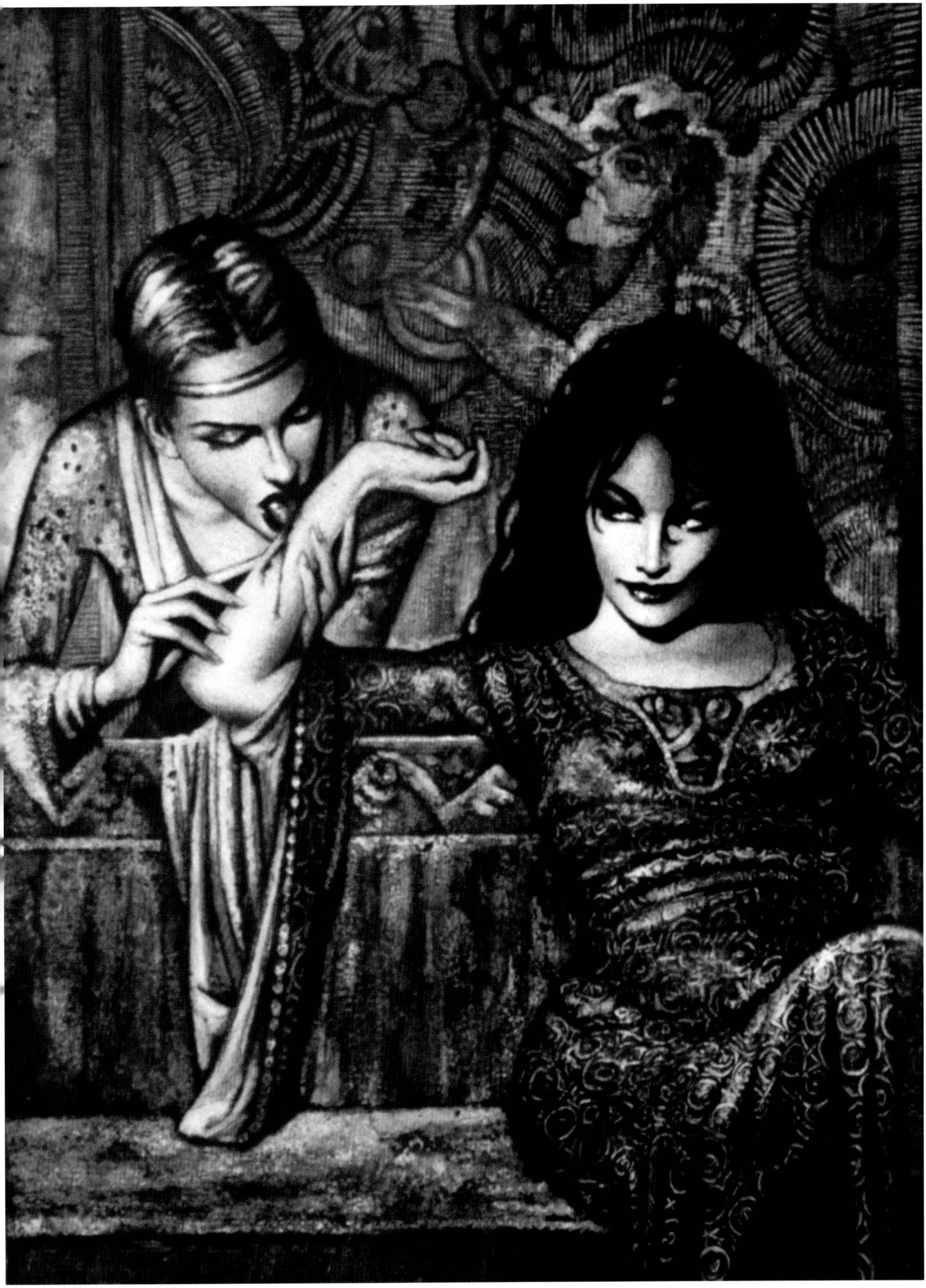

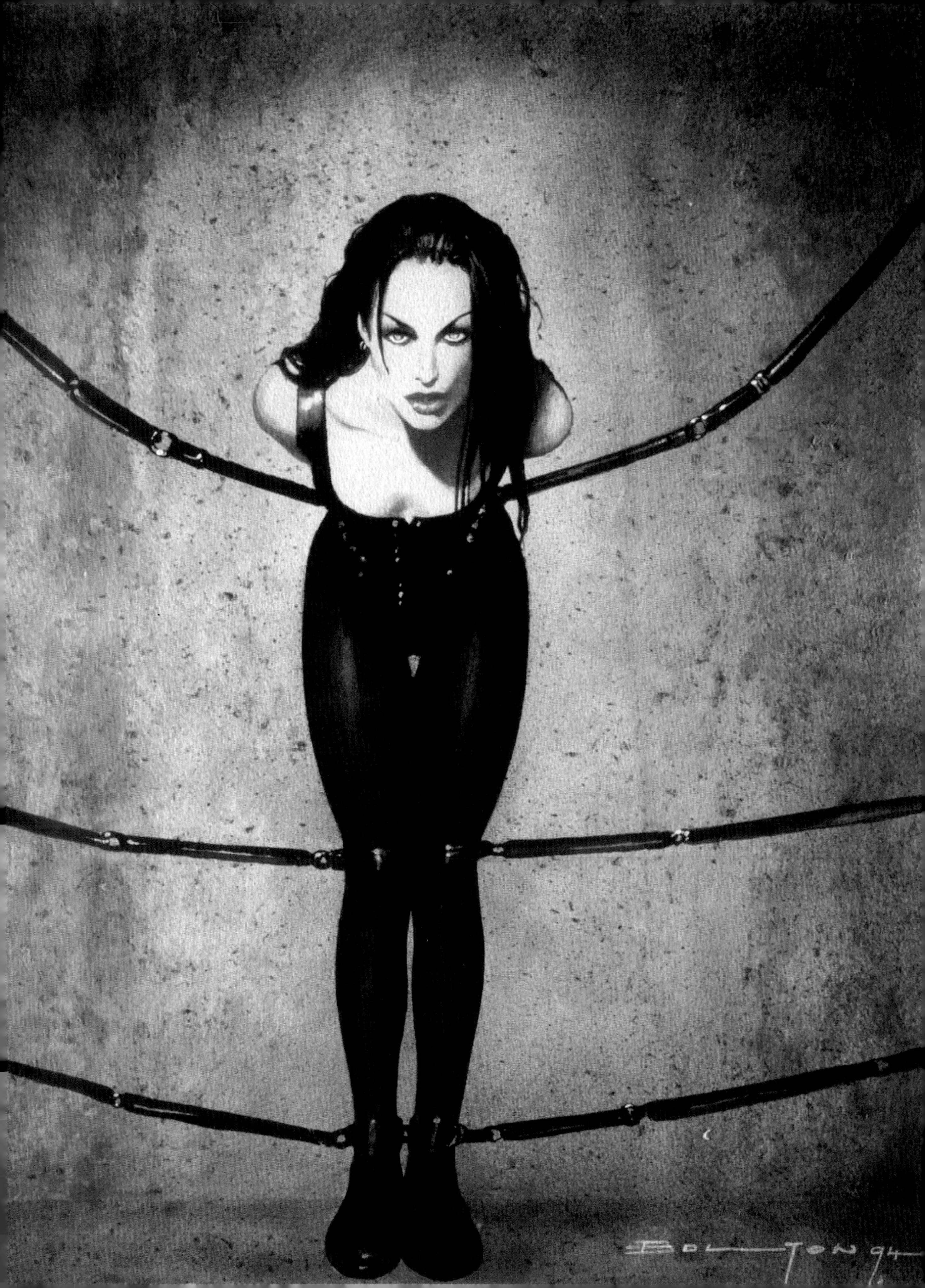
BOLTON 94

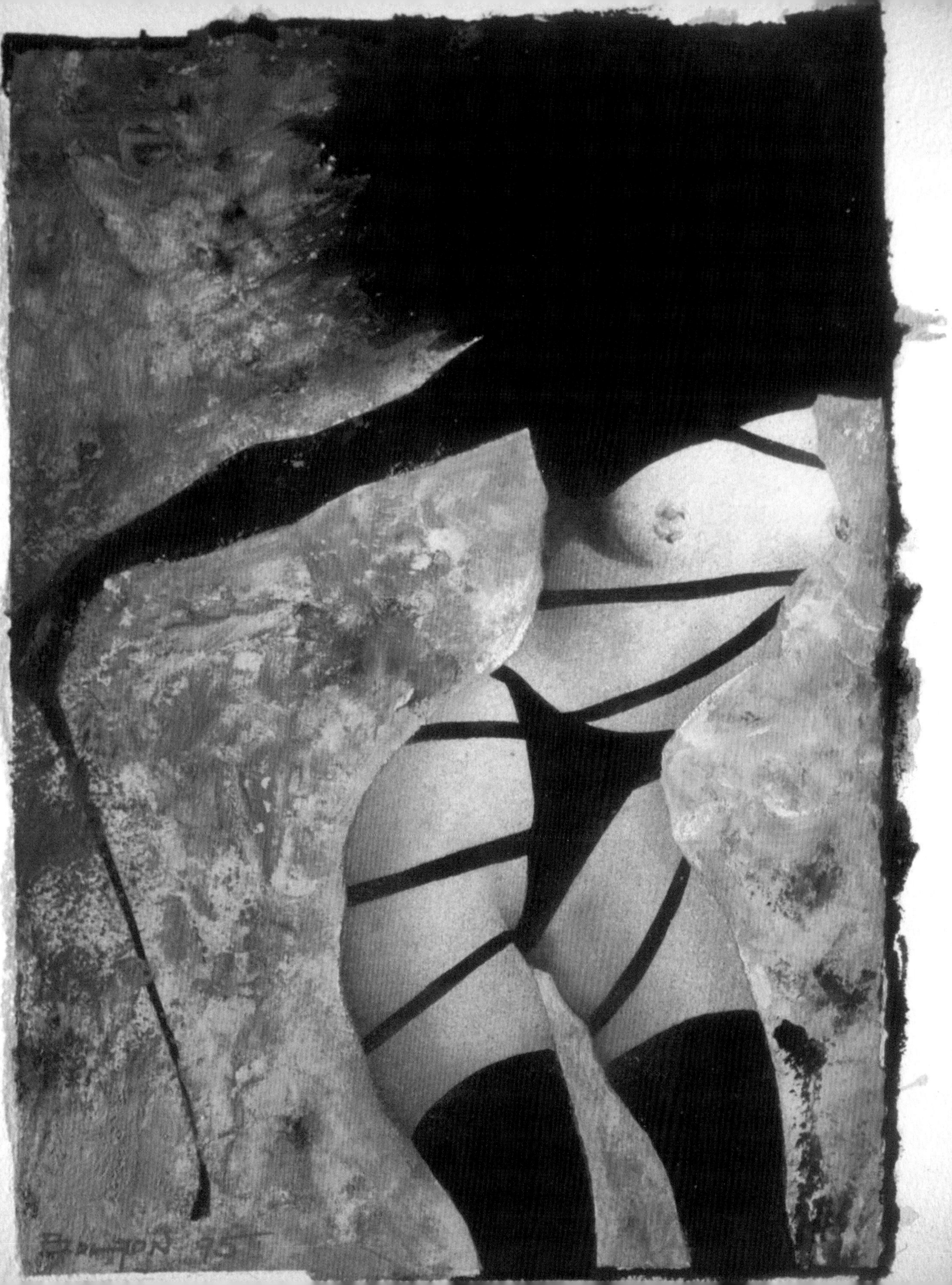

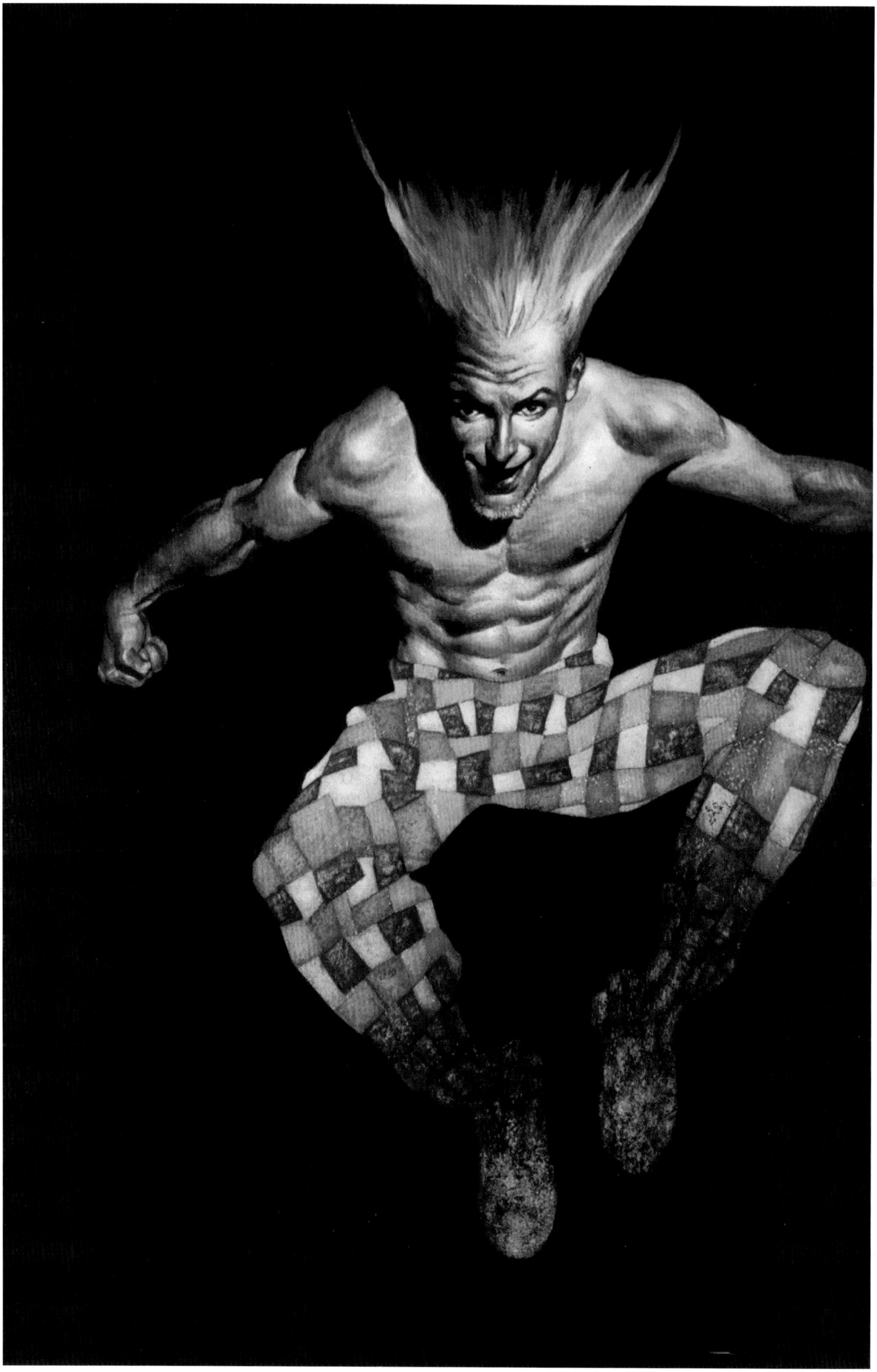

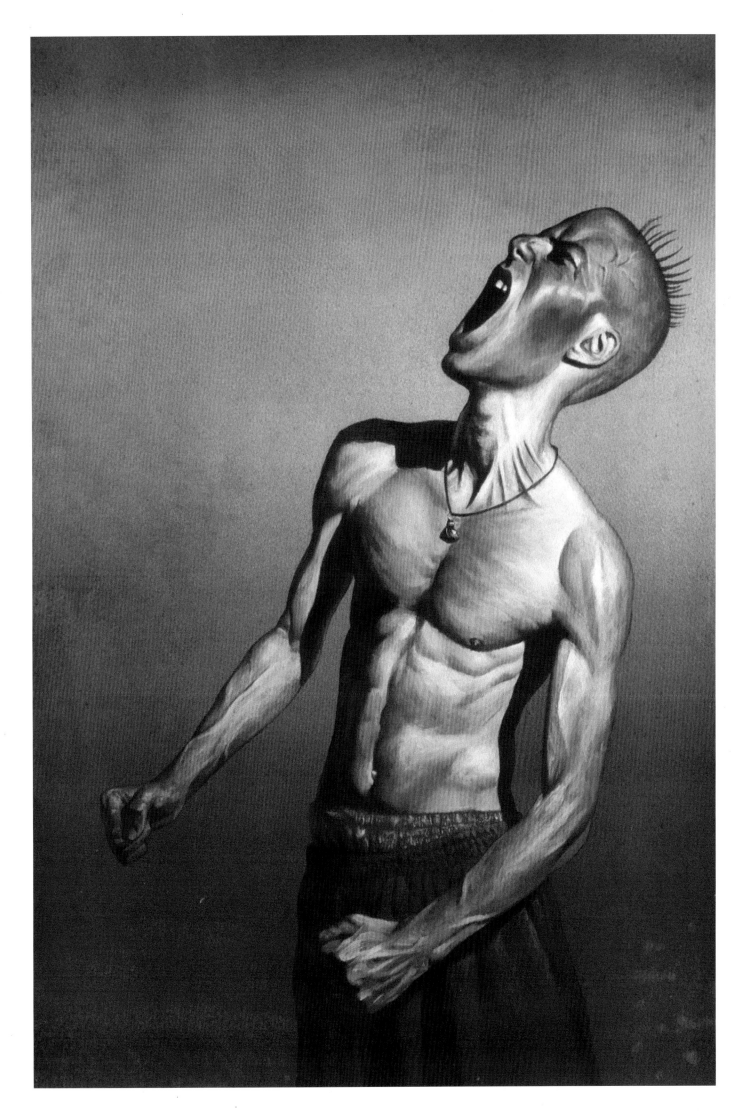

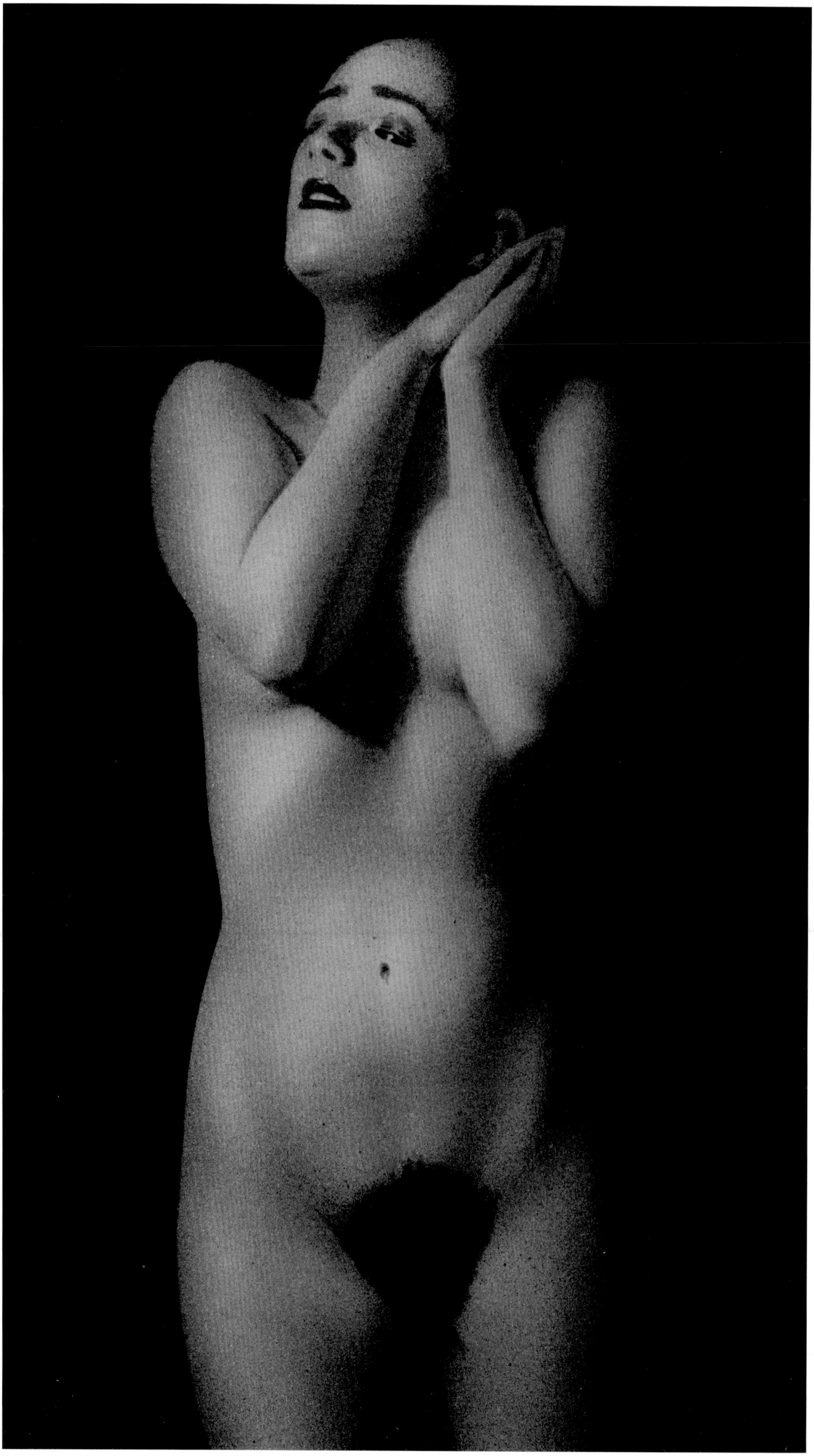

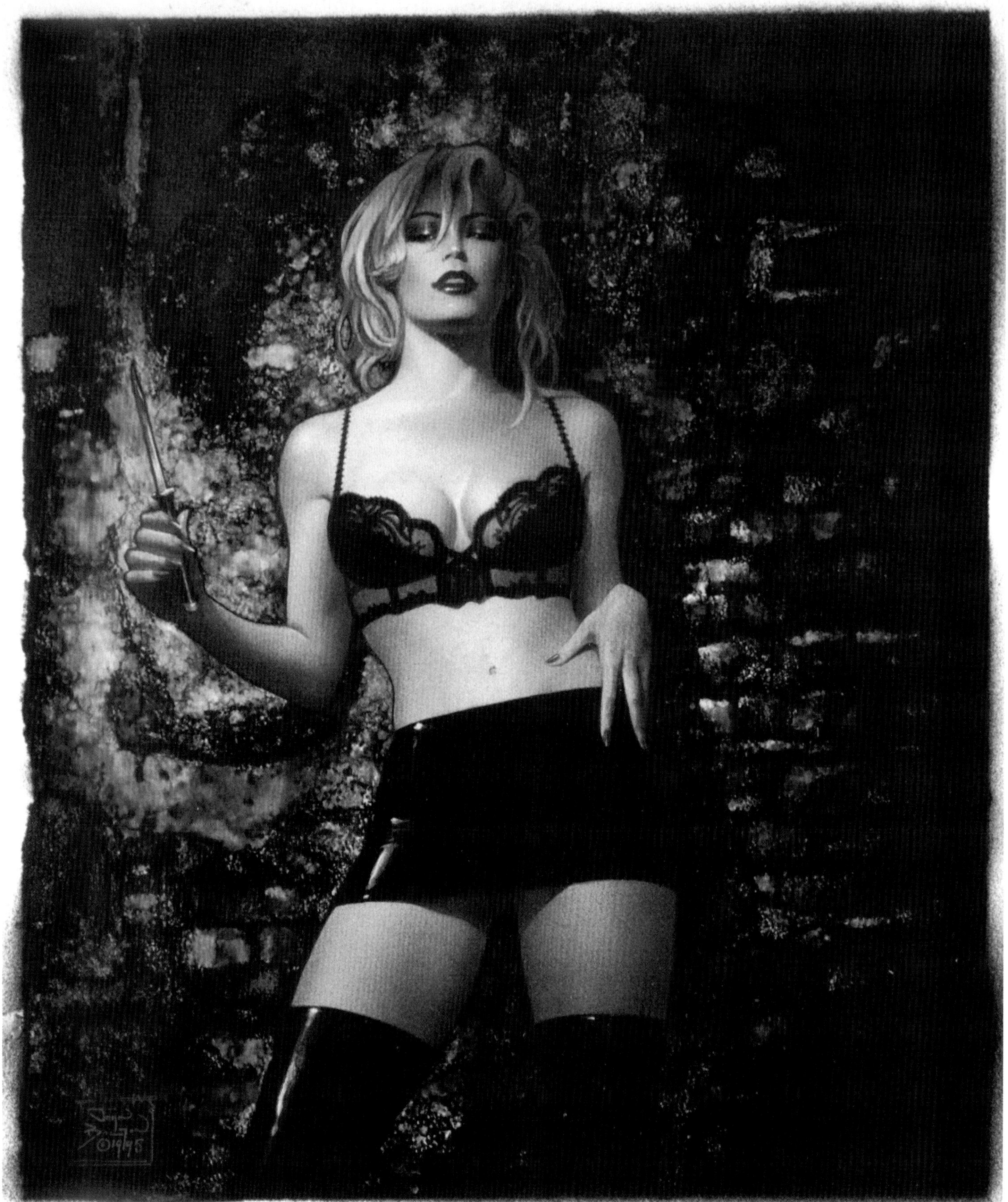

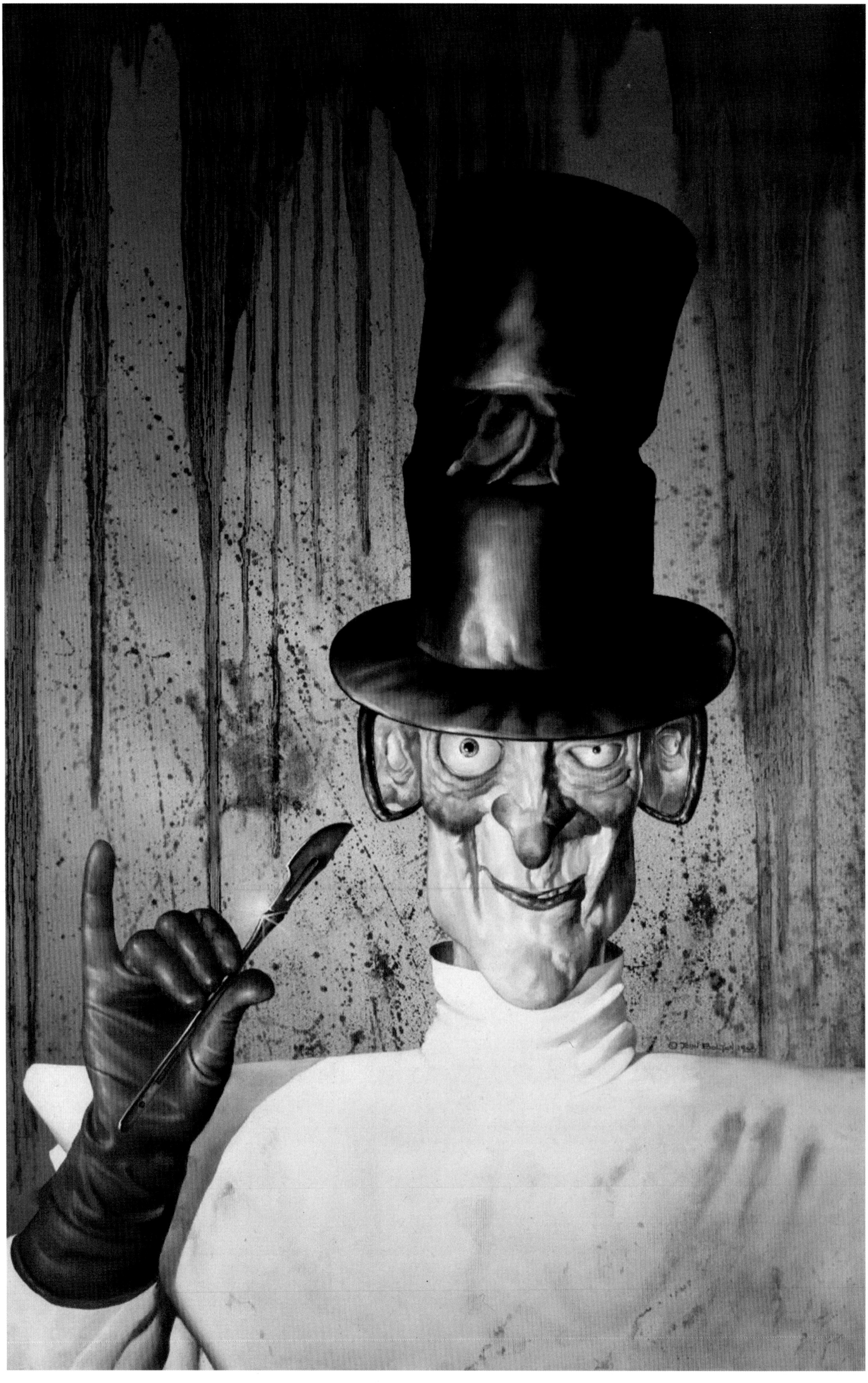

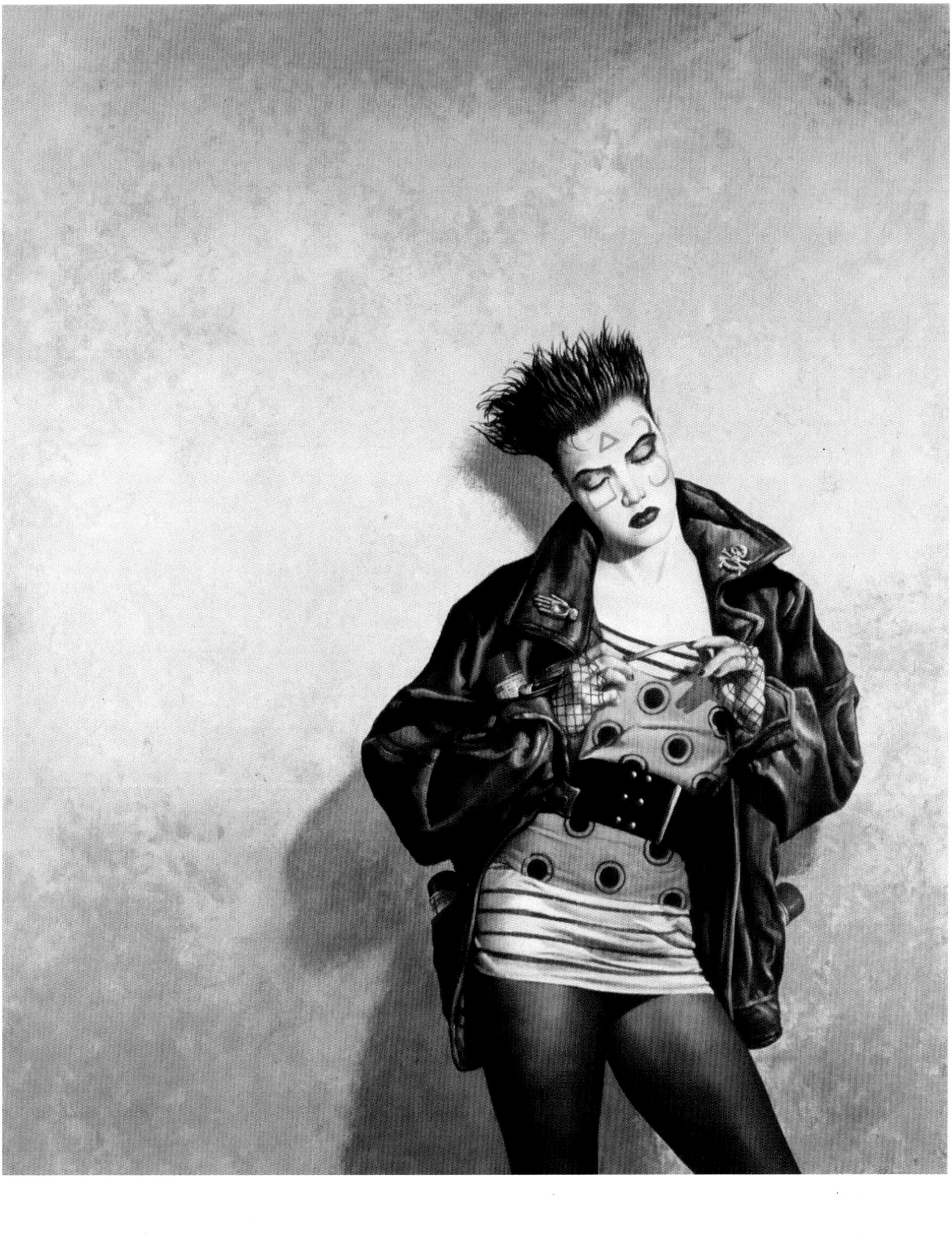

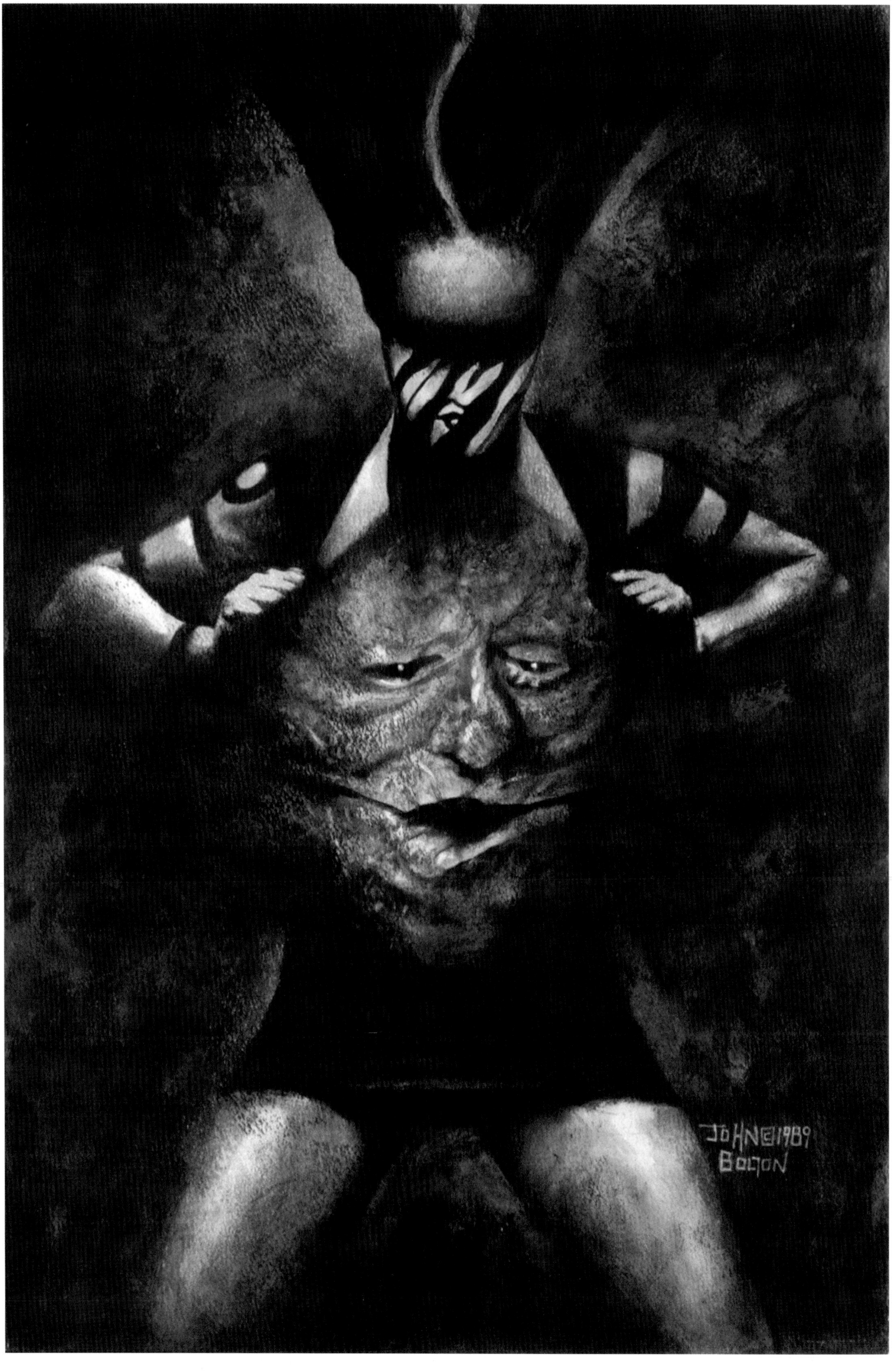
JOHN ©1989
BOLTON

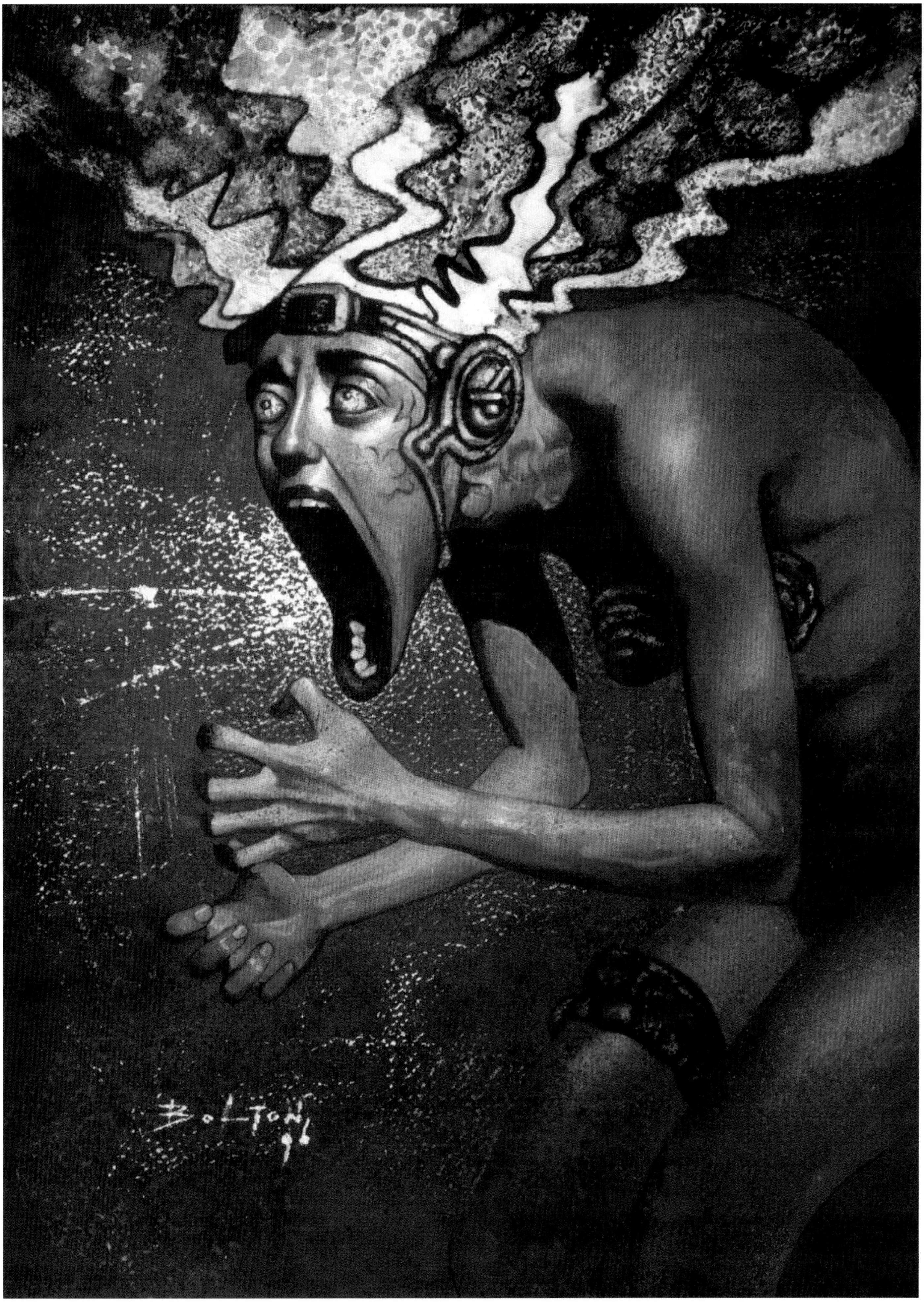
BOLTON 96

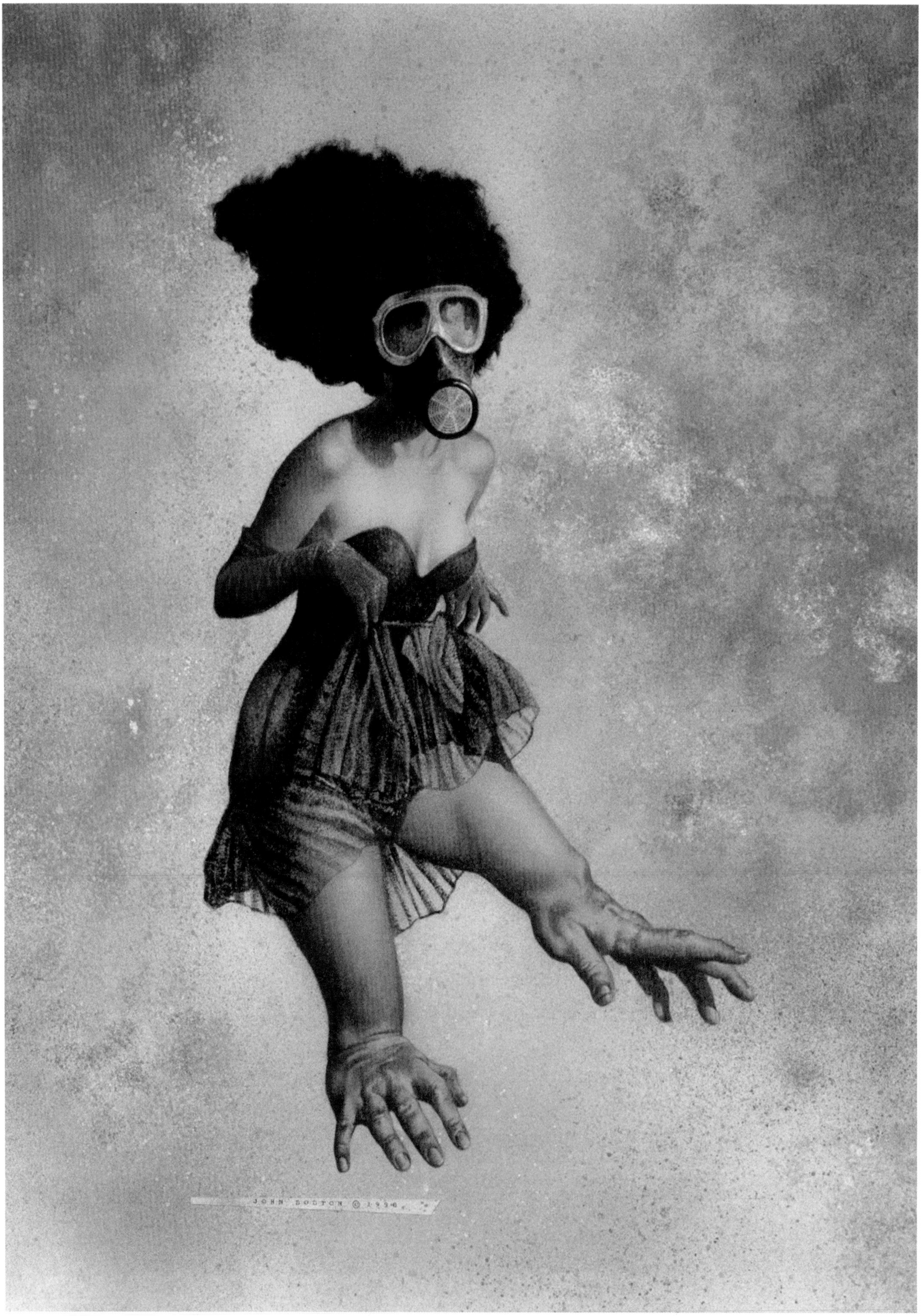
JOHN BOLTON © 1990

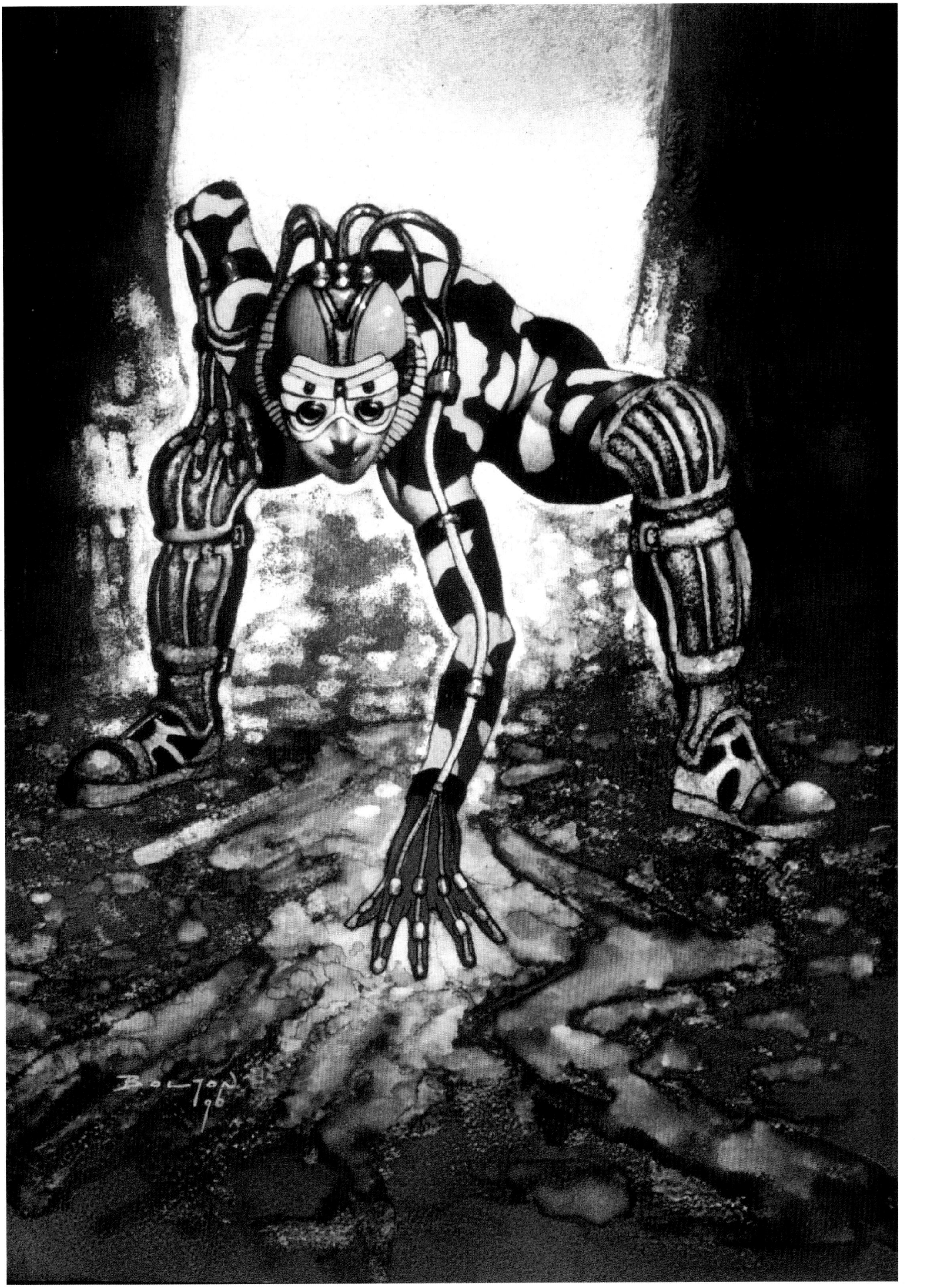
BOLTON
96

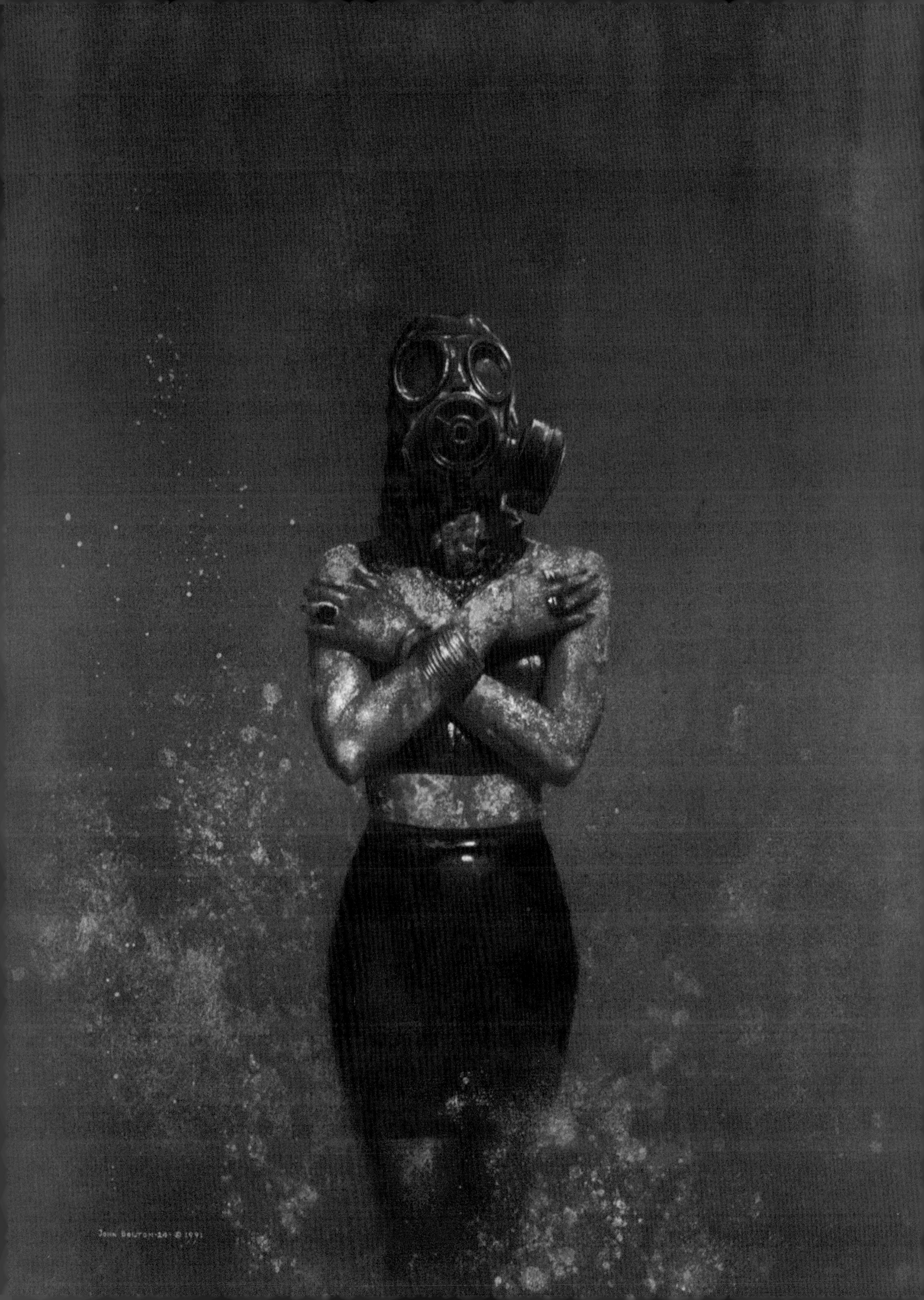

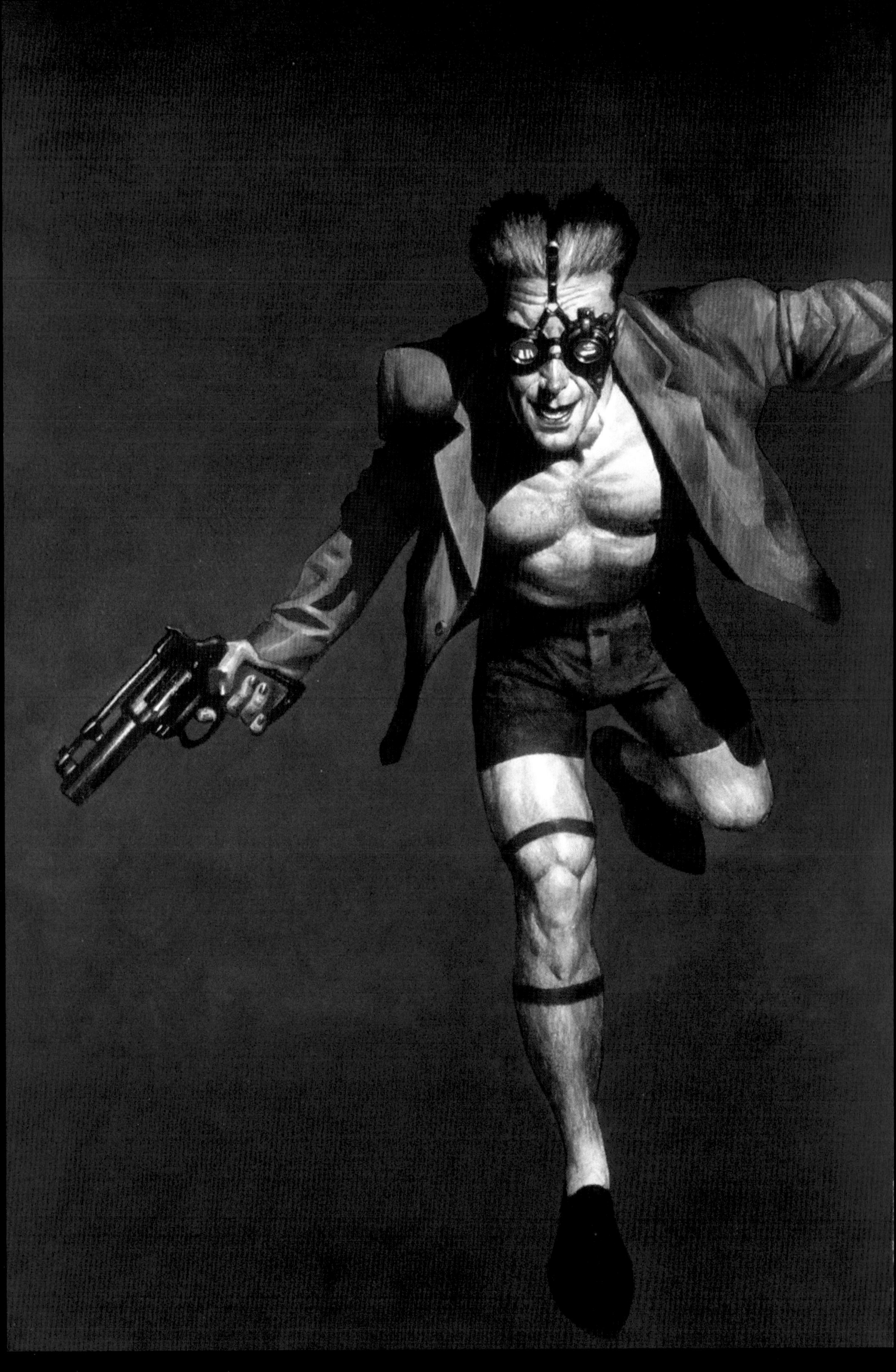

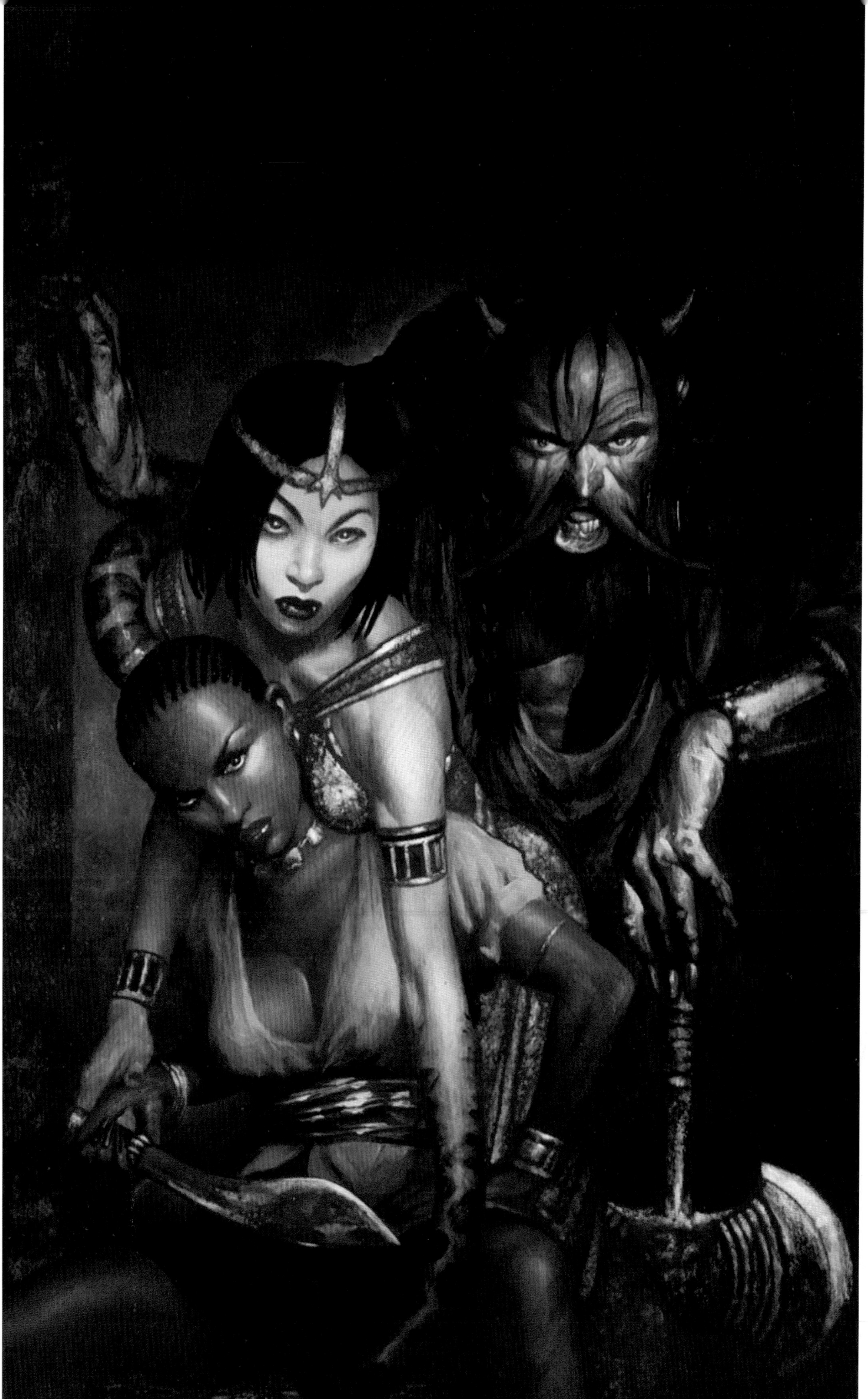

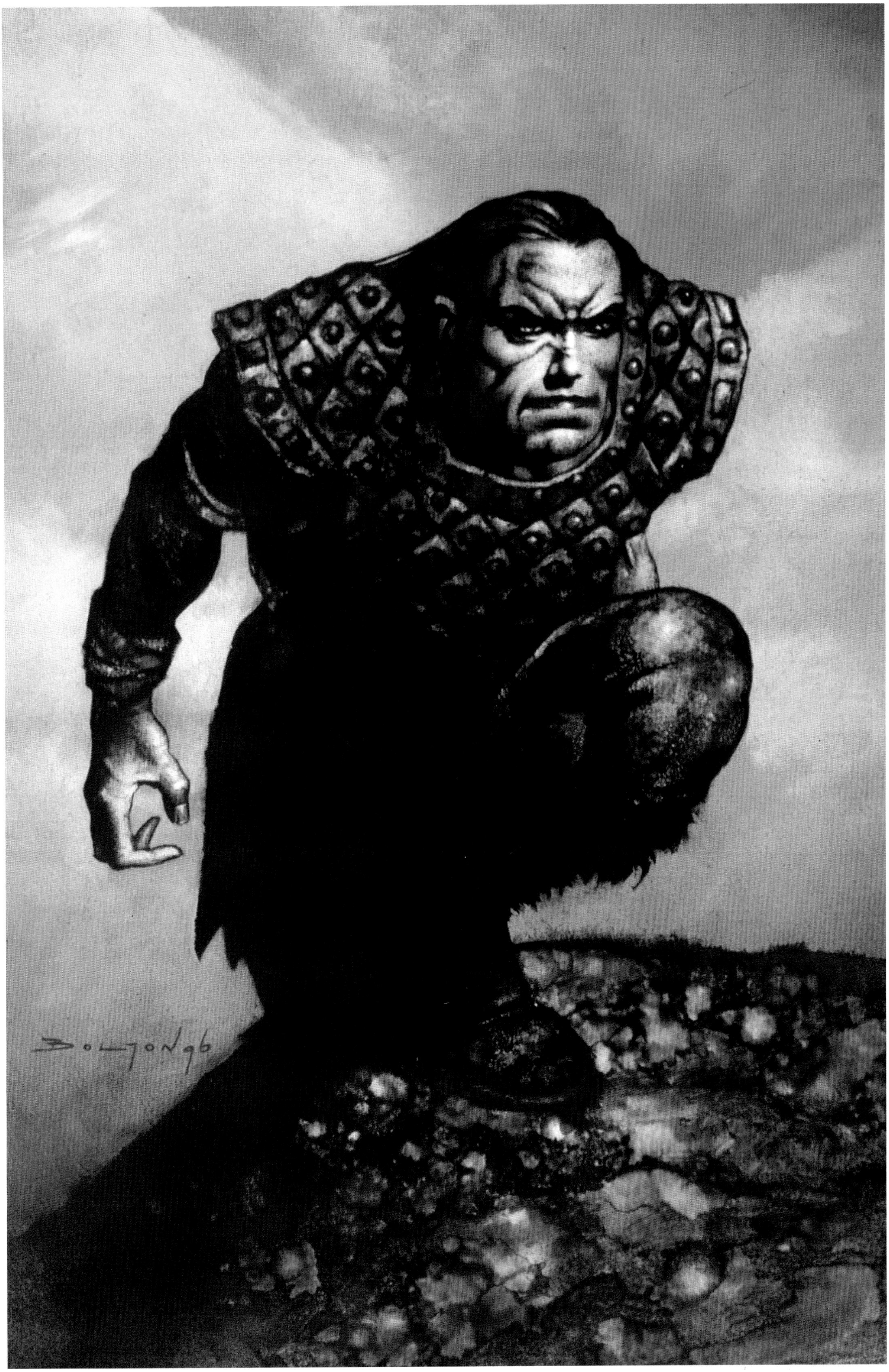
BOLTON 96

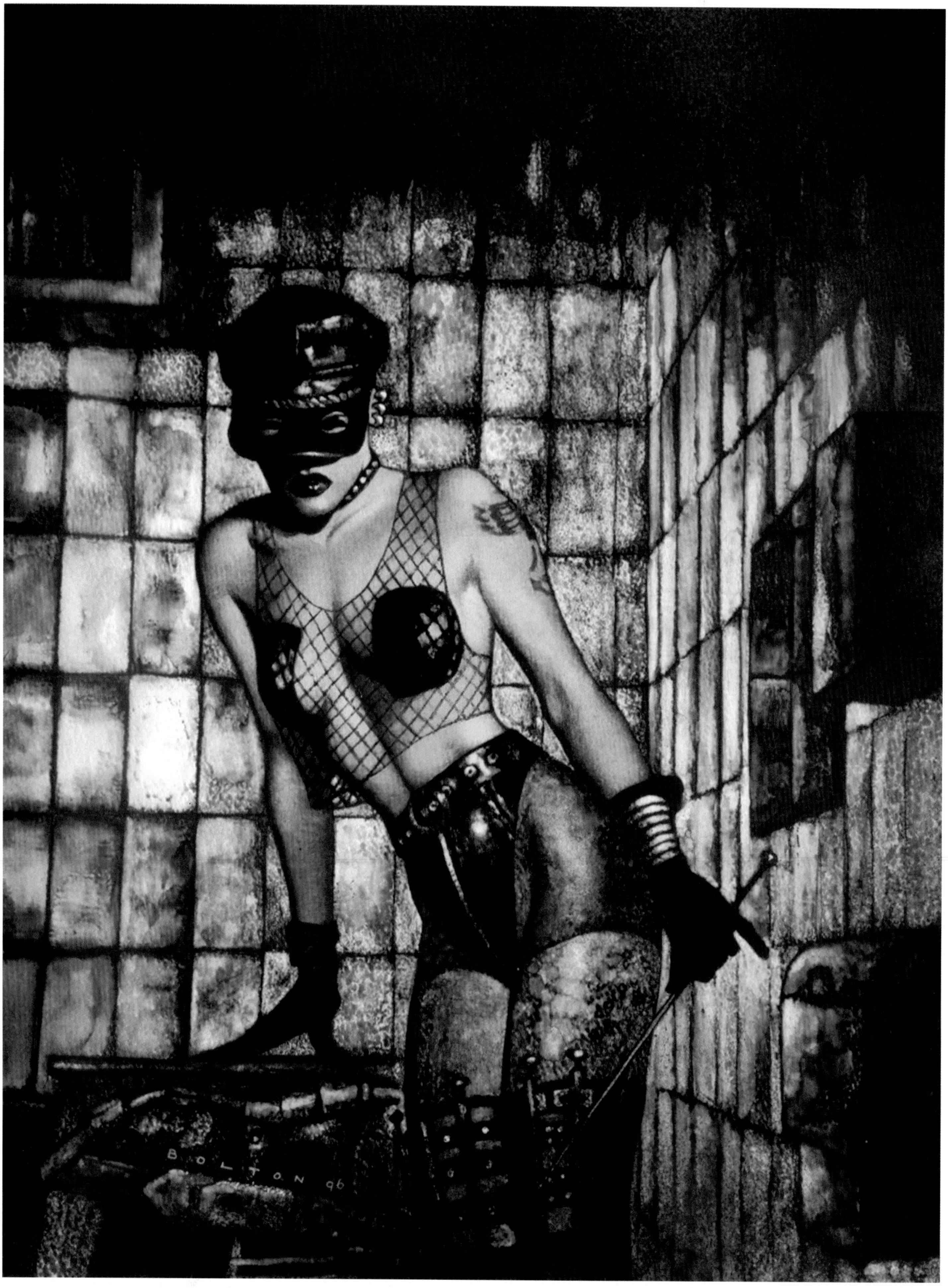
BOLTON 96

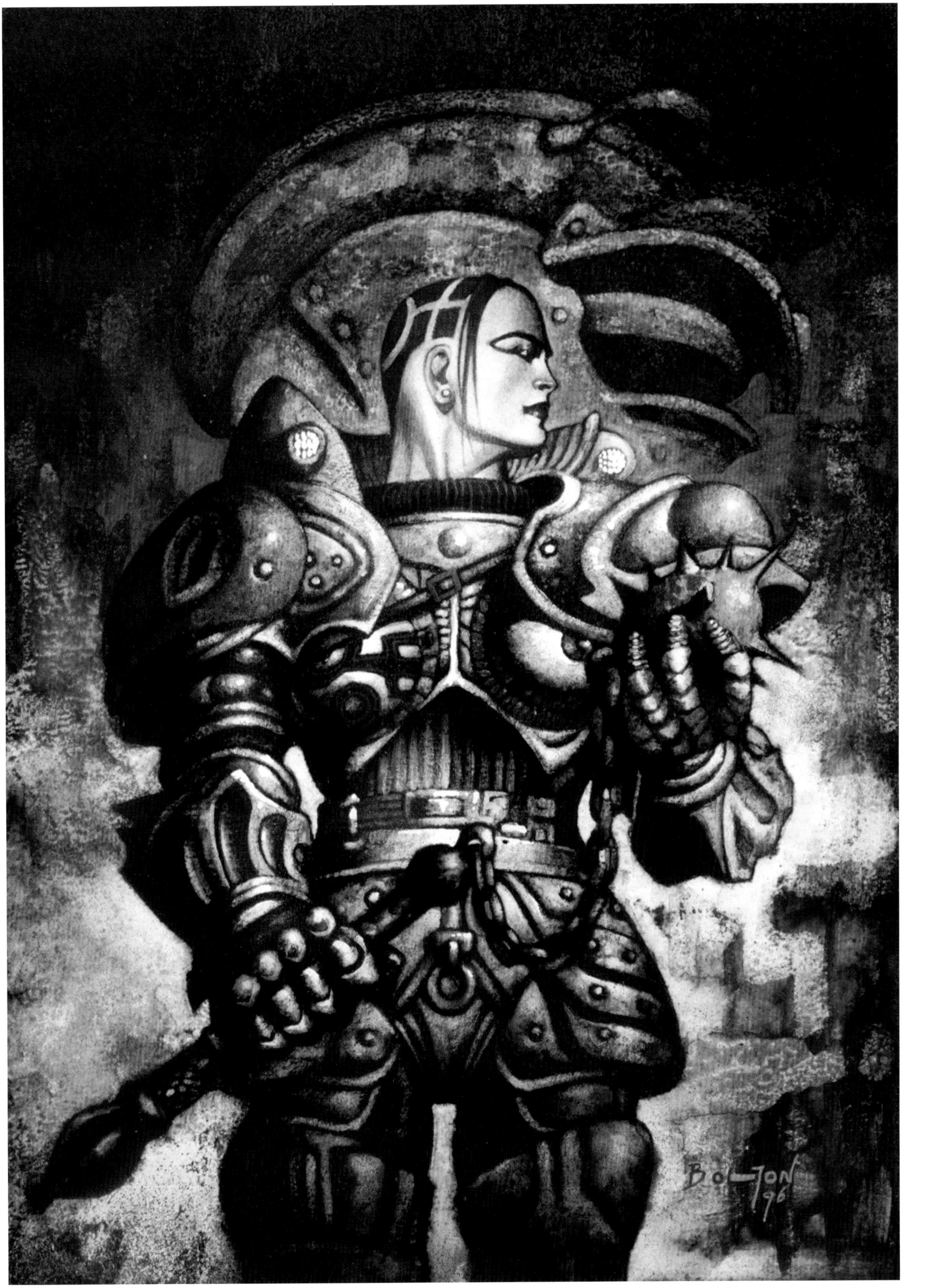
BOLTON
96

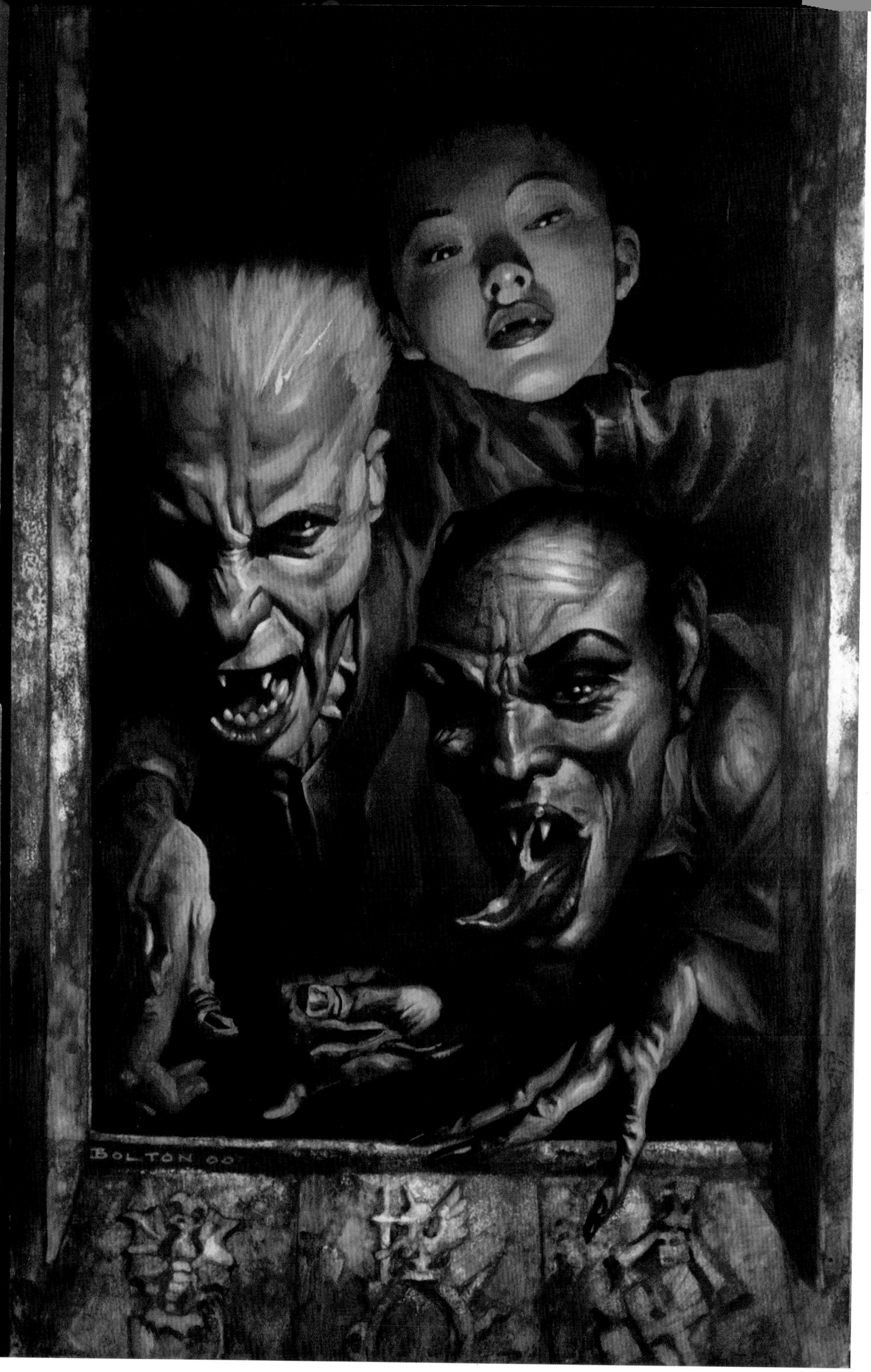
BOLTON 00

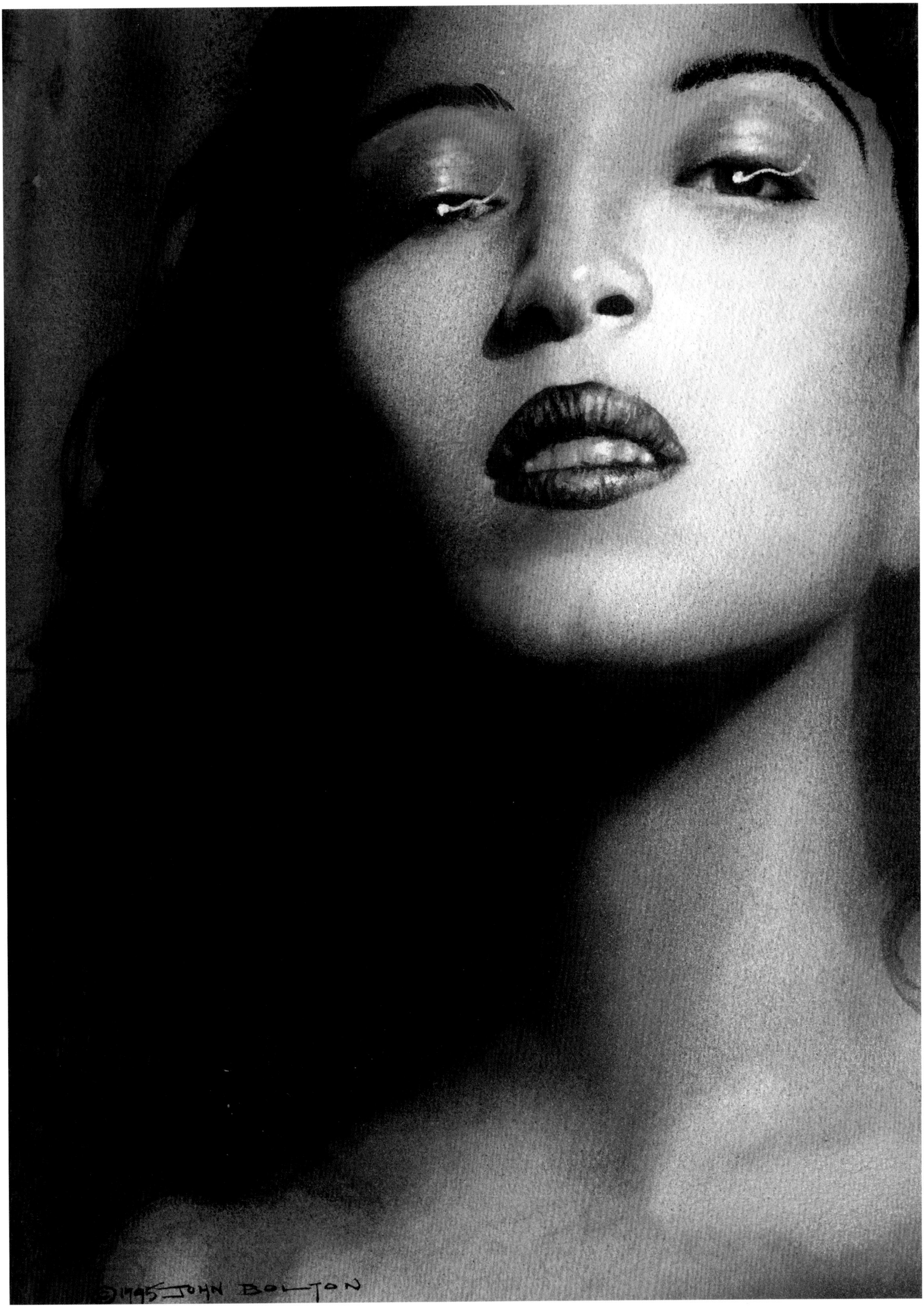
©1995 JOHN BOLTON

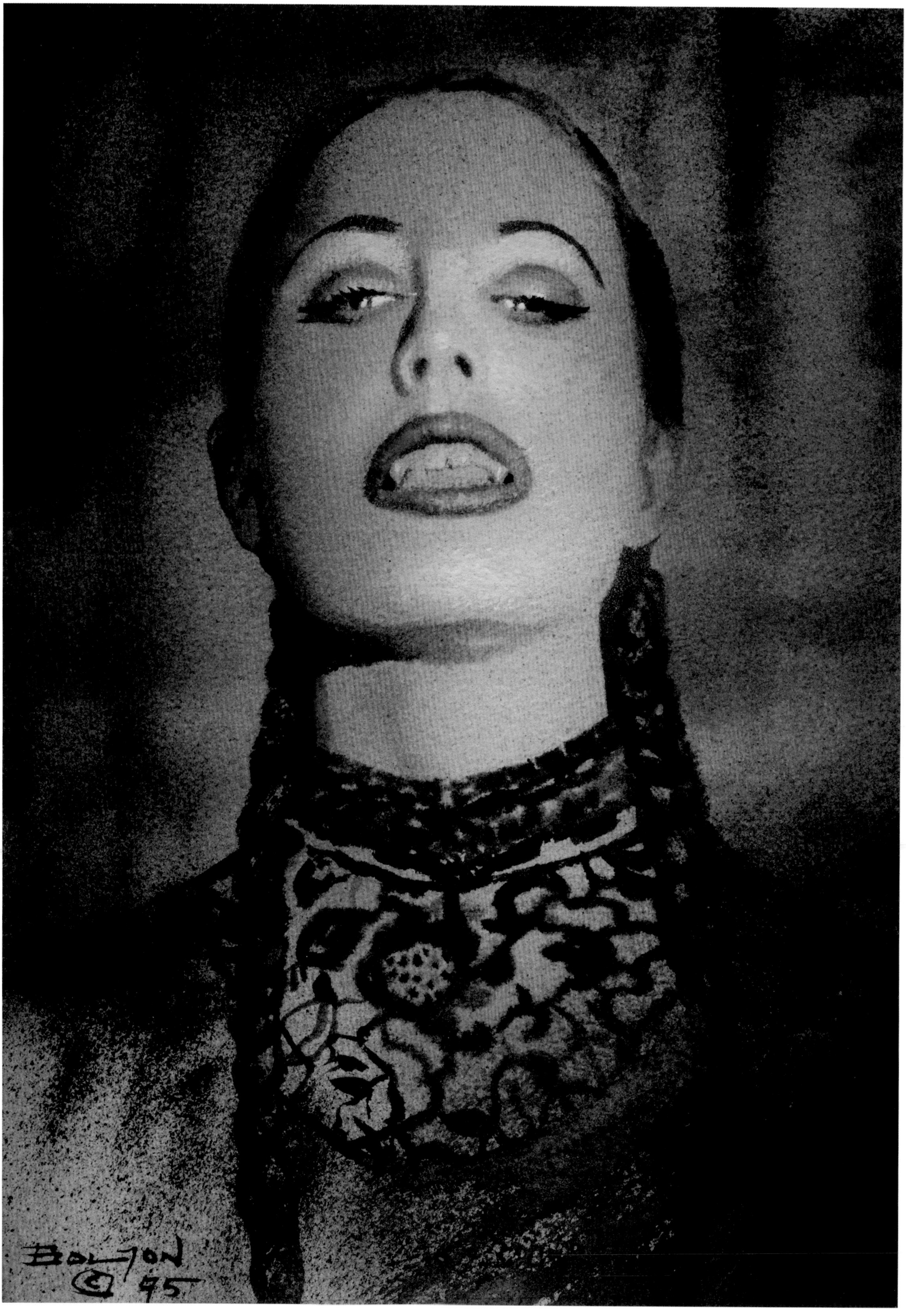
BOLTON
© 95

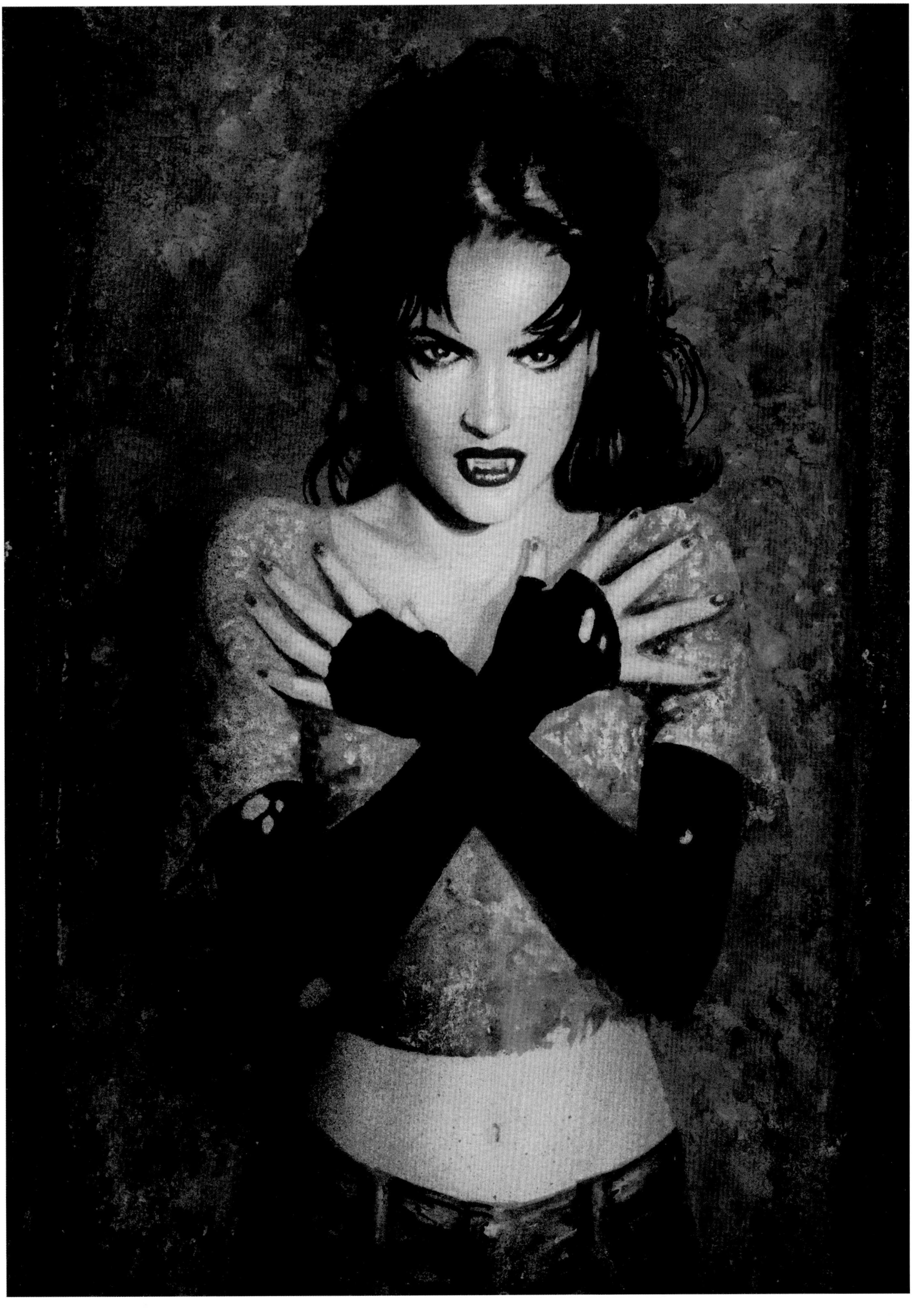

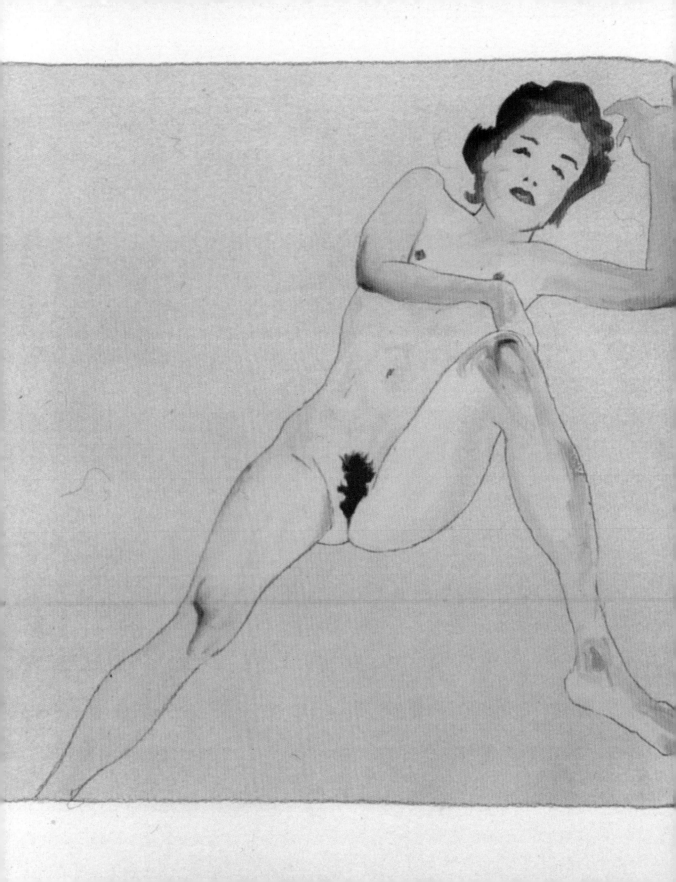

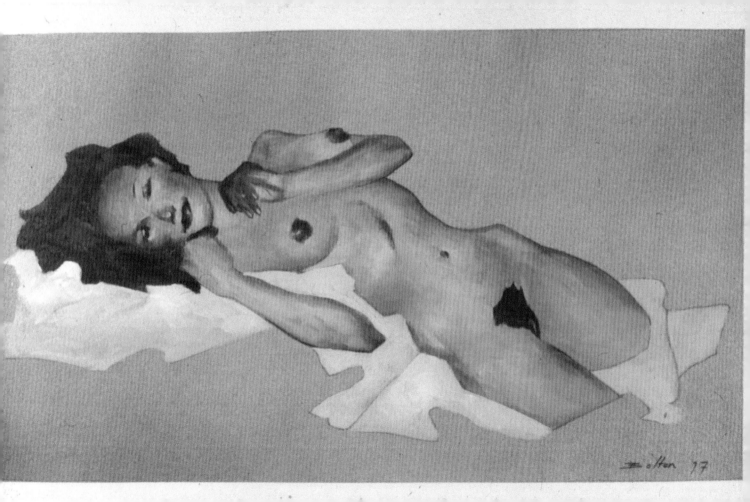

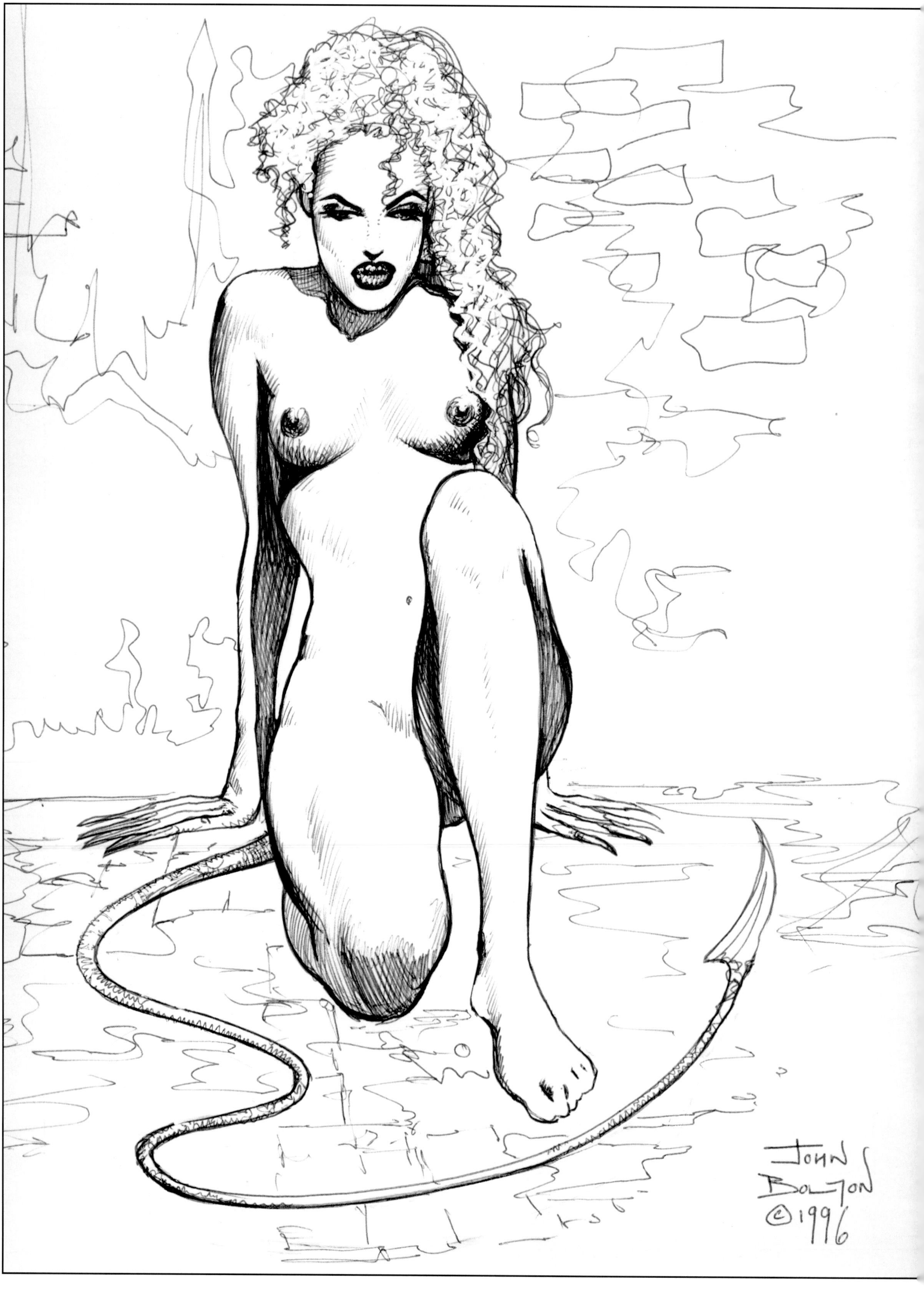
JOHN
BOLTON
©1996

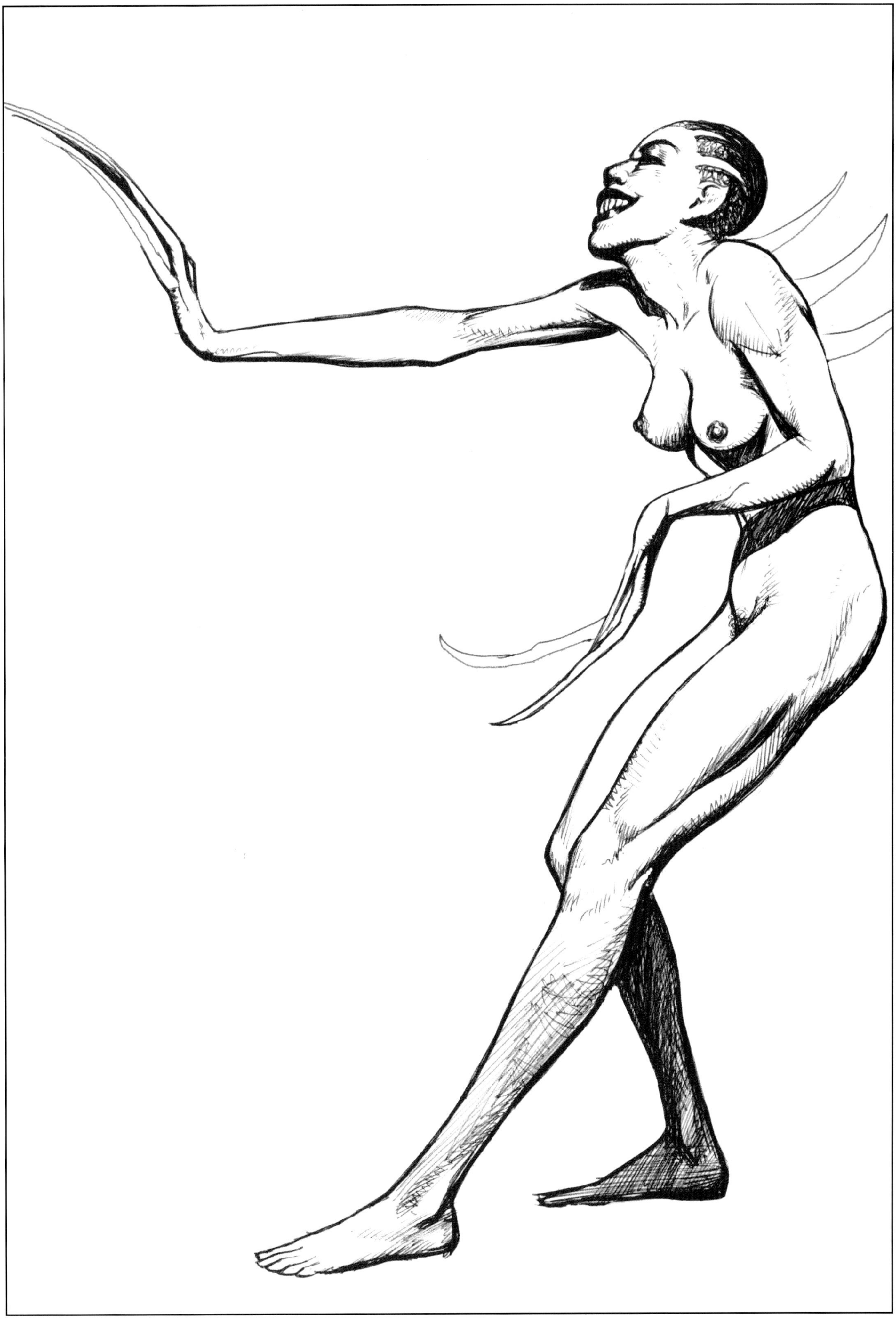

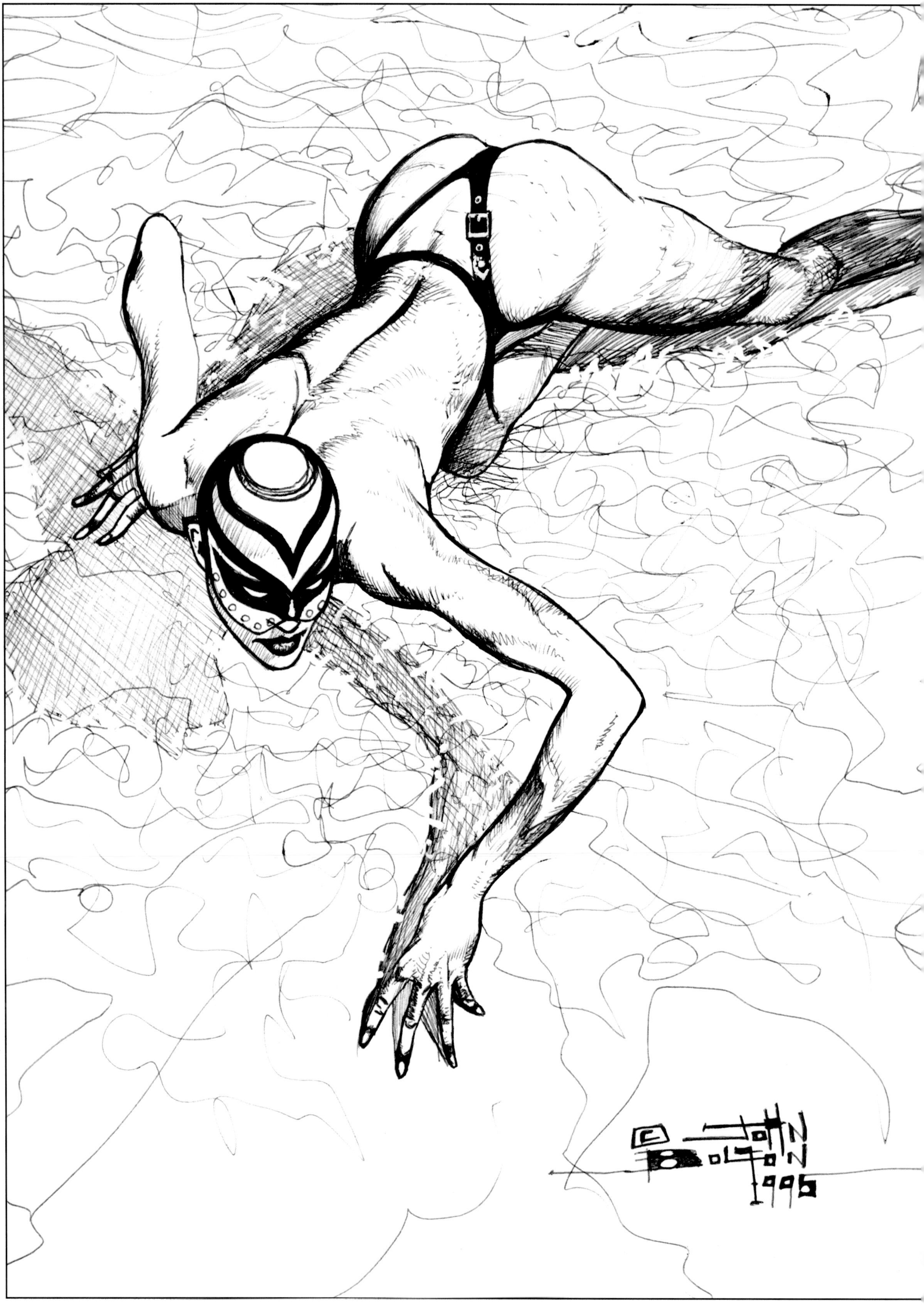
© JOHN BOLTON 1996

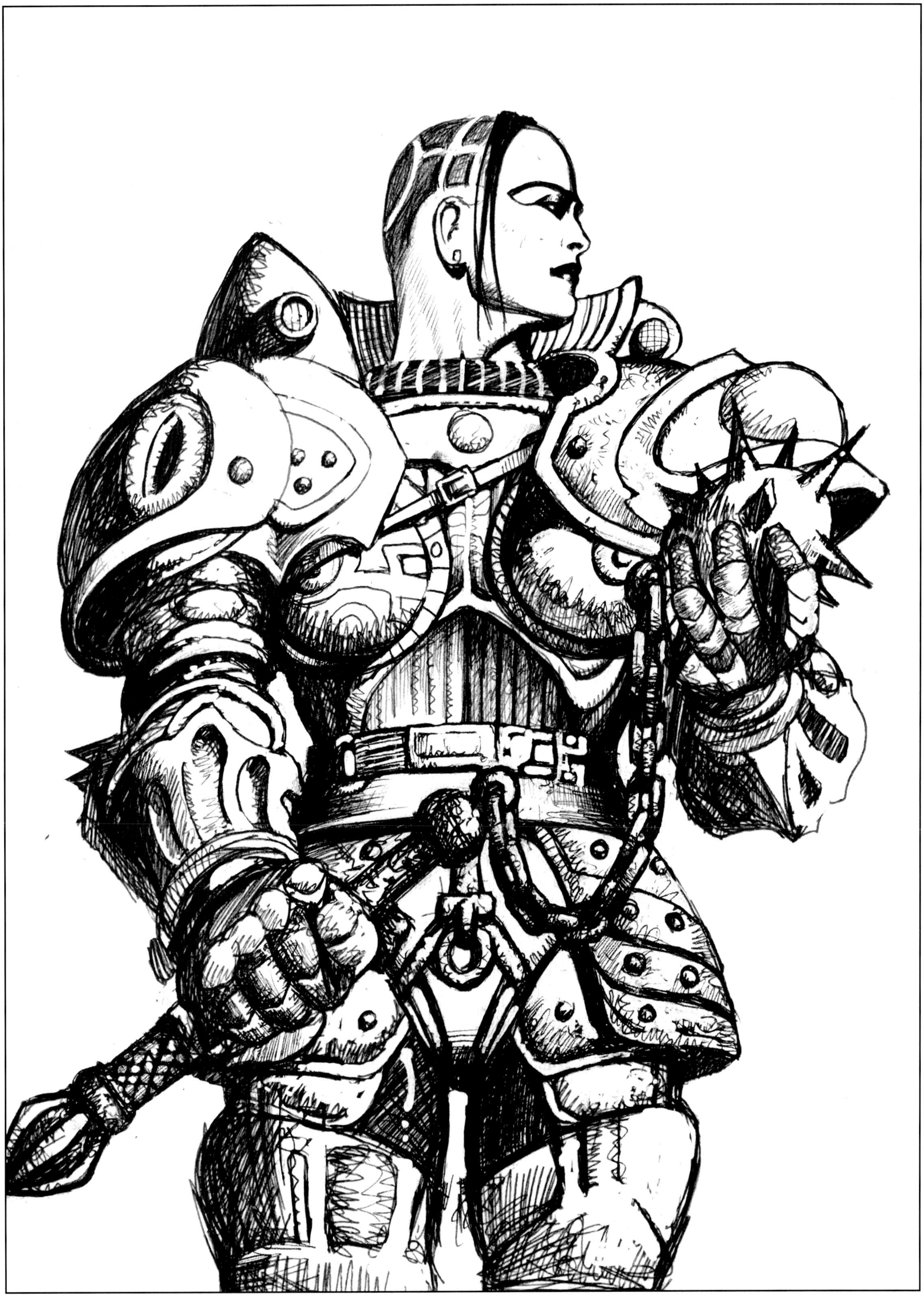

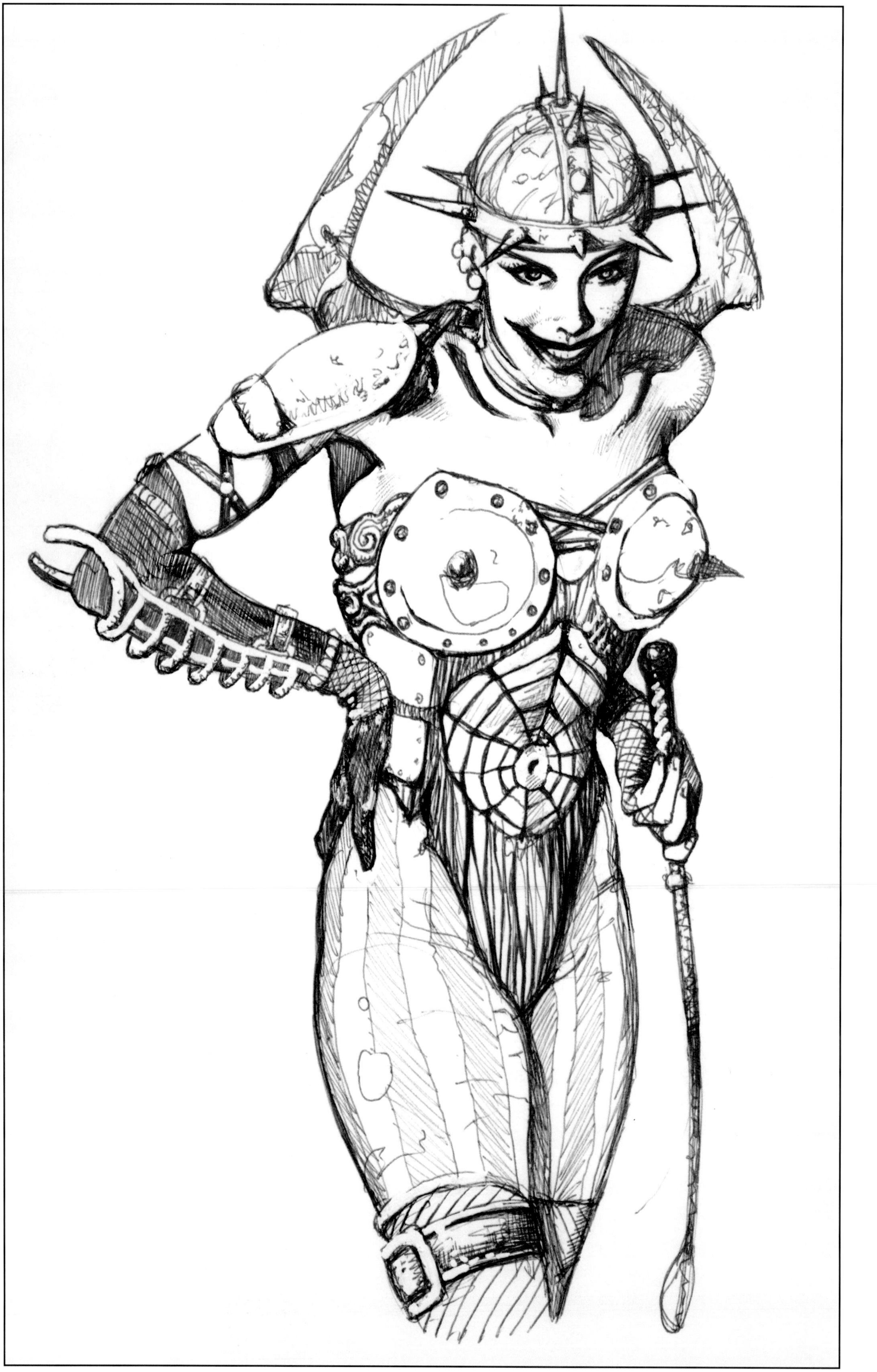

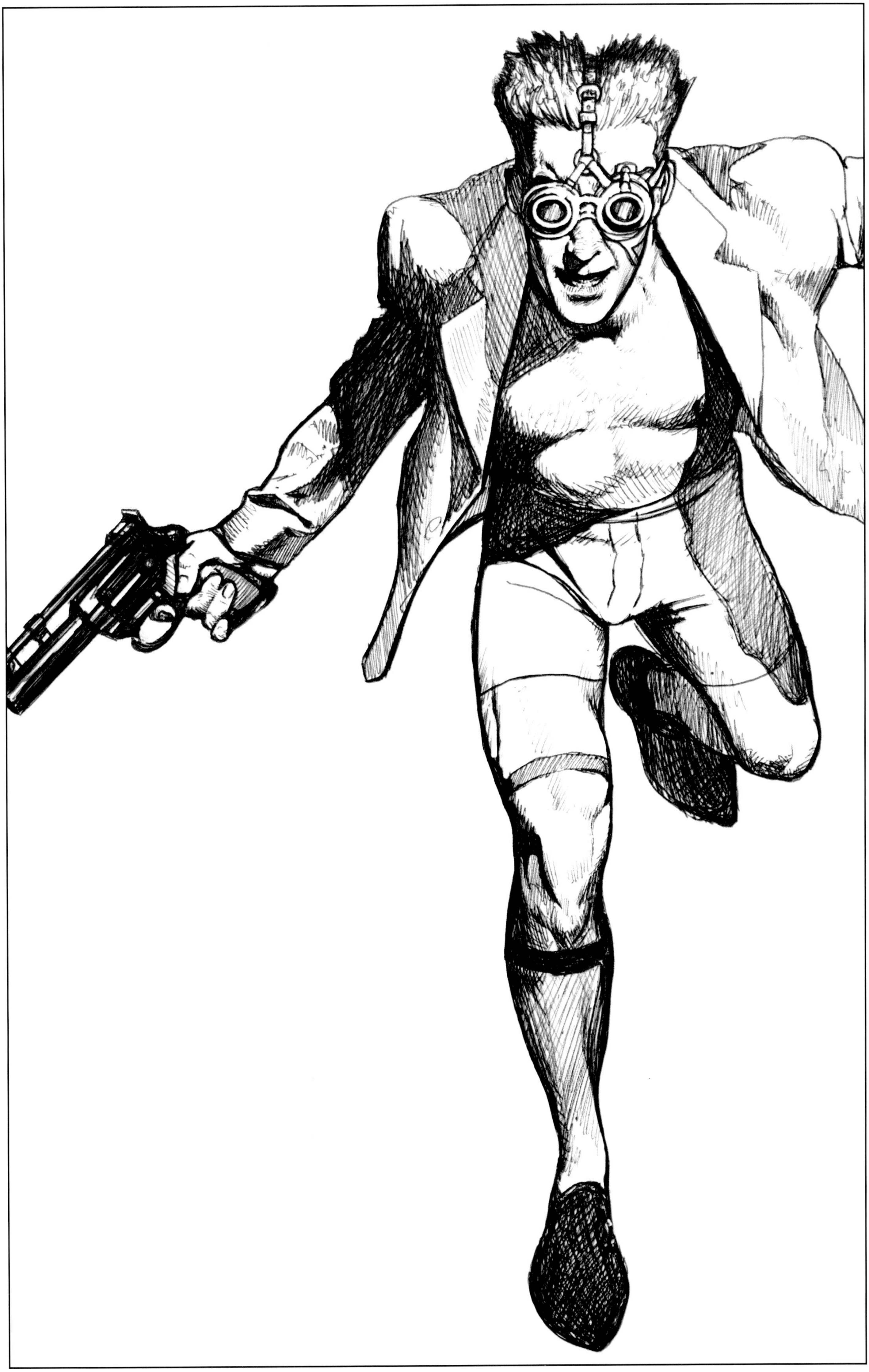

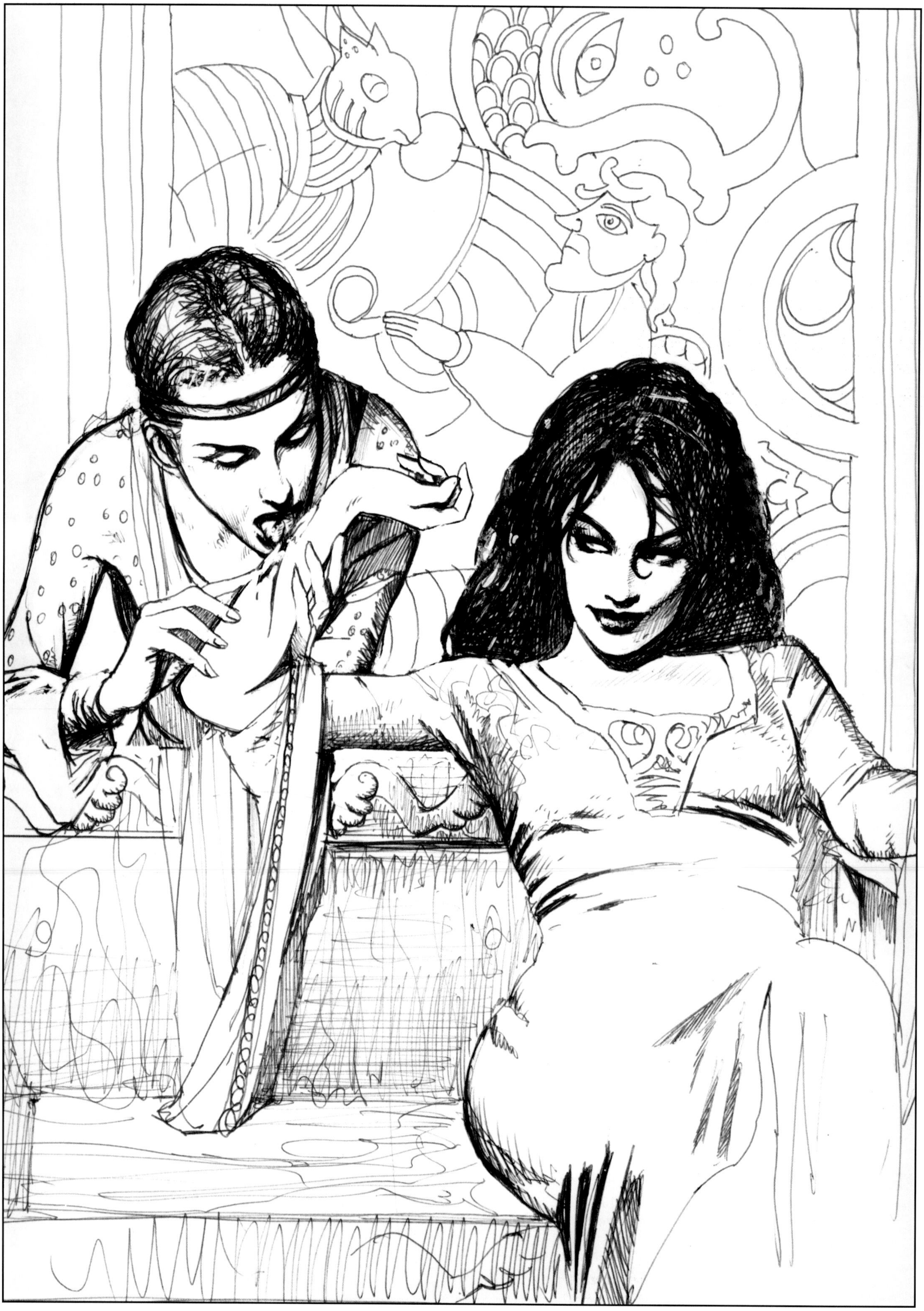

Index

www.johnbolton.com

The official website of John Bolton offers many features, such as information and news about the artist, a short biography, e-mail contact, information about shows he is visiting and of course many of his works. The gallery is subdivided into the section "Aliens", "Vampires", "Roleplaying" and "Comics". There is also information about the official fan club and other art books of the artist. Check out the online presence of the man of whom H.R. Giger once said: "The greatest painter of aliens, beside myself." Enjoy his work!

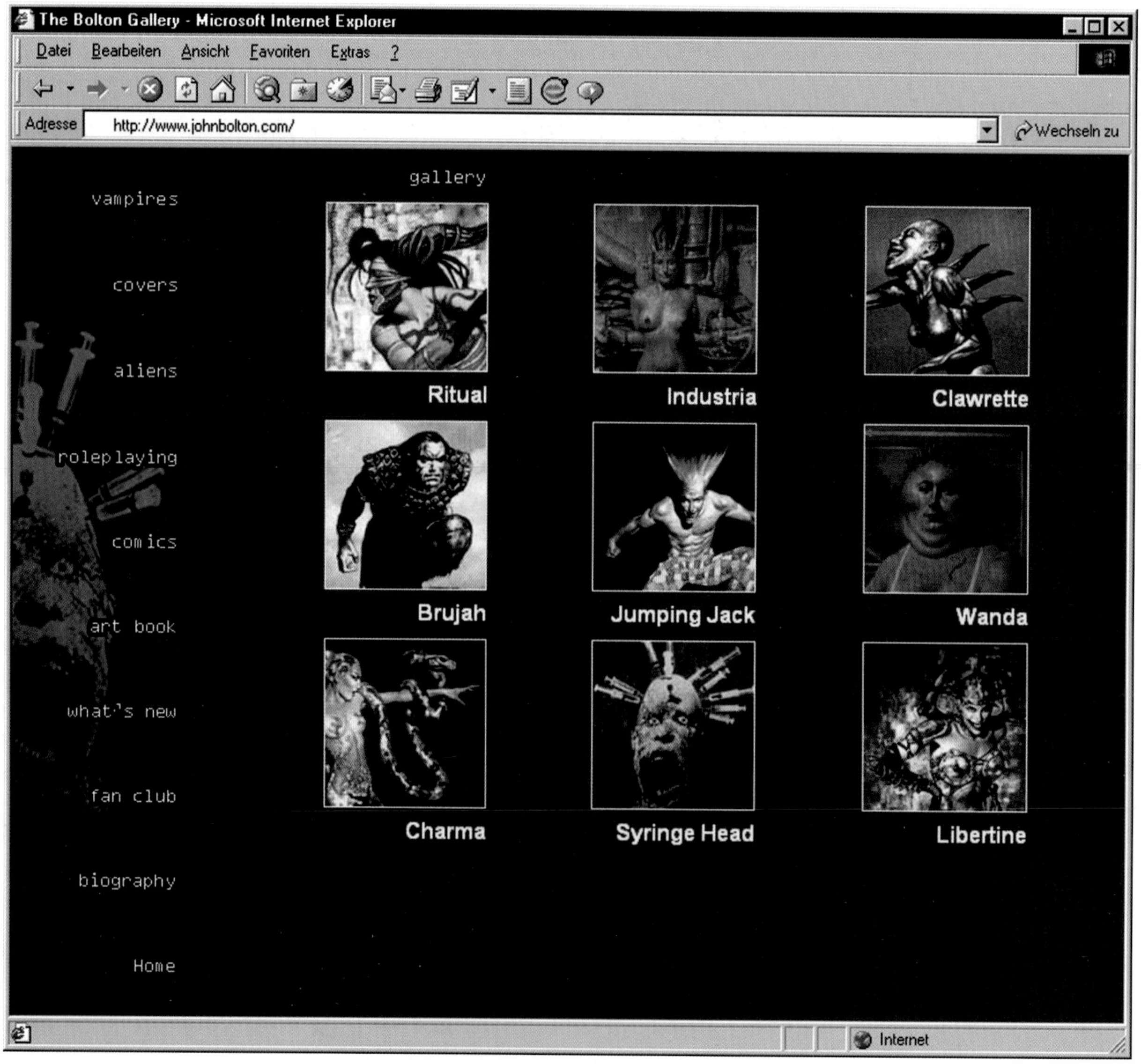
The Bolton Gallery - Microsoft Internet Explorer
Datei Bearbeiten Ansicht Favoriten Extras ?
Adresse http://www.johnbolton.com/
Wechseln zu
gallery
vampires
covers
aliens
roleplaying
comics
art book
what's new
fan club
biography
Home
Ritual
Industria
Clawrette
Brujah
Jumping Jack
Wanda
Charma
Syringe Head
Libertine
Internet